Acquiring Japanese Companies

To my wife, Naomi

Acquiring Japanese Companies

Mergers and Acquisitions in the Japanese Market

Kanji Ishizumi

Basil Blackwell

The first edition of this book (under the title
*Acquiring Japanese Companies: A Guidebook for Entering the
Japanese Market through M & A,* © 1988 by Kanji Ishizumi) was
published by The Japan Times Limited. English rights for this revised
edition arranged with The Japan Times Limited through Japan
Foreign-Rights Centre.

This edition first published 1990.

Basil Blackwell, Inc.
3 Cambridge Center
Cambridge, Massachusetts 02142, USA

Basil Blackwell Ltd
108 Cowley Road, Oxford, OX4 1JF, UK

Library of Congress Cataloging in Publication Data
Ishizumi, Kanji.
Acquiring Japanese companies: mergers and acquisitions in the Japanese
market / Kanji Ishizumi. – Rev. ed.
p. cm.
ISBN 0-631-17716-7
1. Consolidation and merger of corporations – Japan.
2. Investments. Foreign – Japan. I. Title.
HD2746.5.I84 1990
658.1'6–dc20 90-286 CIP

British Library Cataloguing in Publication Data
A CIP catalogue record for this book is available from
the British Library.

Typeset in 11 on 14.5 pt Palatino by
Archetype, Stow-on-the-Wold, Gloucestershire
Printed in Great Britain by
T. J. Press, Padstow, Cornwall

Contents

Contents

Foreword:
Japan is Now Truly an
Open Market

by
Michio Watanabe

Japanese firms are now increasingly active in acquiring American and European businesses, reflecting recent economic trends including the sharp appreciation of the Japanese yen, further internationalization of Japanese firms, and their increasing need for overseas manufacturing operations. On the contrary, however, I have heard of very few cases of acquisition by American or European firms of Japanese companies. By international standards, it is unhealthy for any nation to have a unilateral flow of capital, whether in the form of acquisitions of businesses or assets, or real estate and other investments. The same is true of international trade. I believe that it is an established rule of international trade that every nation must maintain a well- balanced inflow and outflow of capital, goods, and services.

From 1980 to 1982 I held the office of Minister of Finance in the Suzuki Administration, and from 1985 to 1986 that of Minister of International Trade and Industry in the Nakasone Administration. During both terms of office, I encouraged my staff at the ministries to examine existing laws, orders, regulations, and administrative directives, particularly the Foreign Exchange and Foreign Trade Control Act, for any evidence of barriers which might prevent or discourage foreign firms or investors from acquiring Japanese firms: if any remained, staff were instructed to take whatever action might be necessary to remove them. As a result, I believe that there no longer exists any impediment in the Japanese legal system which might prevent foreign firms or investors from acquiring Japanese companies.

I believe that we must now establish an awareness in the business communities of the free nations, including the United States and the nations of Western Europe, that Japan is a fully open market; not only for trade but also as a capital and financial market. Unfortunately, there still seem to be many businessmen in America or Europe who erroneously believe that legal restrictions make it impossible for them to acquire Japanese firms. I hope and believe that this book will help to correct that misunderstanding.

The degree of ease with which firms or investors can make international acquisitions is, in my opinion, one of the practical scales on which free market accessibility can be measured. I recommend this book, in the belief that it will help the Japanese business community and its American and European counterparts to work more closely together and perhaps to fuse into one.

Michio Watanabe is a former Minister of Finance and Minister of International Trade and Industry. He represents the Liberal Democratic Party in the House of Representatives, and is Chairman of the party's Political Affairs Research Committee.

Preface to the First Edition

"Is it possible for foreign corporations or investors to purchase and hold shares in Japanese corporations with a view to acquisition?" "Is it true that if foreign corporations or investors attempt to acquire Japanese corporations, the Ministry of International Trade and Industry (MITI) and/or the Ministry of Finance (MOF) will intervene and exercise their/its power in the form of *gyosei shido* (administrative guidance or advice) to frustrate the attempt?" "Does the Japanese Antimonopoly Act make it difficult for foreign corporations or investors to acquire Japanese firms?" "Where can I get professional advice in Japan if I want to acquire a Japanese corporation?"

I have been asked these questions hundreds of times by American and European business executives, most of whom believe the answers will be negative and that it is extremely difficult, if not altogether impossible, for them to establish a presence in the Japanese market through the acquisition of an existing Japanese firm. But they are wrong. Believing that it is necessary to correct these and other misunderstandings, which are harmful not only to Japan but also to the US and Europe, I have written this book to help foreign business executives and corporate lawyers to gain an accurate view of the current environment for mergers and acquisitions in Japan.

Recently, as Japanese firms have begun to acquire American and European corporations, a number of books have been published specifically to provide Japanese businessmen with the practical information that they need. Among these was my book *Kokusai kigyo baishu handbook* (Handbook on international mergers and acquisitions, published in 1987 by Toyo Keizai

Shimposa Ltd). But to the best of my knowledge this is the first book written in English from inside the Japanese business community to explain to foreign readers the practical, methodological, tactical, strategic, and procedural aspects of mergers and acquisitions in Japan. I pride myself that this book is not only original and path-breaking but also timely.

In writing the book, I have tried to explore as many past merger and acquisition cases as possible, so as to provide foreign readers not only with accurate and complete information on all aspects of mergers and acquisitions in Japan, but also with a proper understanding of Japanese corporate culture and the ways in which the emotions and mental reactions of Japanese business executives differ from those of their American or European counterparts when their companies become acquisition targets. I hope and believe that this book will be accepted and used by American and European businessmen, investment bankers, and lawyers as a practical guidebook for dealing with Japanese business executives in merger and acquisition scenarios.

Japan has long been a net importer of books, particularly those on business and law. I hope that this book will go some way to reducing Japan's huge trade deficit in this sector.

Kanji Ishizumi

Abbreviations

CEO	chief executive officer
CPA	certified public accountant
FEFT	Foreign Exchange and Foreign Trade Control [Act]
FTC	Fair Trade Commission
FY	financial year
GNP	gross national product
M & A	mergers and acquisitions
MITI	[Japanese] Ministry of International Trade and Industry
MOF	[Japanese] Ministry of Finance
MOJ	[Japanese] Ministry of Justice
MOT	[Japanese] Ministry of Transport
NSC	Nippon Steel Corporation
PBR	price book ratio
PCSE	potential common stock equivalent [ratio]
PER	price earning ratio
R & D	research and development
SEC	Securities and Exchange Commission
TSE	Tokyo Stock Exchange

1

Why Enter the Japanese Market?

The Japanese Ministry of International Trade and Industry (MITI) compiles annual statistics relating to "foreign-capital-based" corporations, defined here as Japanese corporations, doing business in Japan, that have more than 50% of their equity capital or voting stock owned either directly or indirectly by non-Japanese individuals or corporations. According to the 1987 statistics (released in September 1987), the aggregate accumulated amount of direct investment by such corporations in Japan, up to the end of March 1987, reached US$7.0 billion. Of the 2,094 foreign-capital-based corporations doing business in Japan at that time, 894 responded to the survey. Their origins varied considerably: 434 (48.5%) American, 99 (11.1%) Asian, 69 (7.7%) West German, 66 (7.4%) British, 53 (5.9%) Swiss, and 42 (4.7%) French. At the time of the survey, the 894 respondents had some 130,000 employees, 0.4% of the nation's total workforce.

According to the MITI survey of FY 1984, the aggregate amount of capital expenditure made during that year by these 894 corporations reached ¥206.4 billion, which is 3.6% of the aggregate capital expenditure made by the nation's entire manufacturing sector during the year. While 55.6% of the corporations of American origin were engaged in manufacturing, over 60% of those of Asian extraction were engaged in distribution and marketing.

In the fiscal year ending in 1984, the total annual revenue of the foreign-capital-based corporations responding to the survey reached ¥13,595.6 billion, 73.3% of which was accounted for by manufacturing: this percentage represents 3.2% of the total annual revenue reported by the nation's entire manufacturing sector. In addition, the 894 respondents, as a group, earned export revenue totalling some ¥924.9 billion in 1984, representing 2.3% of the nation's total exports of ¥41,184.4 billion. Moreover, their total imports into Japan reached ¥4,908.6 billion, 15% of the nation's total imports of ¥32,661.3 billion. This already substantial share of the Japanese market is expected to continue to increase in the future.

MITI's annual statistics reveal various reasons why foreign-capital-based corporations had decided to maintain a presence or do business in Japan: 41.7% thought that the Japanese market was very attractive and offered a promising future; 17.8% replied that they had come to Japan to establish a base from which to expand into other Asian markets; 11.8% had wanted to take advantage of Japan's highly developed industrial technologies; 7.1% believed that they could procure industrial materials, parts, and components more easily in Japan than anywhere else; 5.8% had been attracted by the apparent absence of significant competition in both Japan and neighboring countries; 3.7% replied that their main interest was the availability of cheap, high-quality labor; and 1.3% replied that it was their intention to take advantage of the country's ample financial resources.

Japan has over 120 million consumers: the Japanese generally have a very keen eye for quality and demand an extremely high level of after-sales service. This is one of the reasons why it is often said that any product which is well received in Japan will be successful worldwide. Japan's *per capita* GNP is immense, second only to that of the United States. Japan is also one of the most highly educated nations in the world, with nearly 35% of

Why Enter the Japanese Market?

young adults going to college – the illiteracy rate is virtually nil. For this reason, the country offers a homogeneously well-trained, skilled labor force.

The Tokyo financial market is one of the world's three largest – comparable in size to that of New York or London – and foreign-capital-based corporations doing business in Japan can make full use of its facilities to satisfy all their financial requirements. It is no overstatement to claim that any American or European corporation that considers itself to be truly international in its outlook must have a presence in Japan, one of the most competitive markets in the world.

The ownership structures of the 894 foreign-capital-based corporations in the MITI annual survey were as follows: 407 (45.5%) were wholly owned either directly or indirectly by non-Japanese corporate or individual investors; 208 (23.3%) were joint ventures between non-Japanese and Japanese corporate or individual investors, with non-Japanese corporate or individual investors owning a majority, but less than 100%, of the shares; and 279 (31.2%) were joint ventures owned equally by non-Japanese and Japanese corporate or individual investors.

The statistics of those Japanese corporations that have become foreign-capital-based through acquisition or joint venture are shown in Tables 1.1 and 1.2. Table 1.1 shows part of the statistics compiled and published by Professor Walter Ames in the *Harvard International Law Journal* in 1986. In his paper, he states that, as of the end of 1984, there were 5,786 Japanese corporations which had foreign capital participation and that 684 (11.8%) of these had been set up as purely Japanese corporations, but had subsequently become owned, either wholly or partially, by non-Japanese corporate or individual investors.

Table 1.1 shows Japanese corporations which have become foreign-capital-based since 1955, with a majority of their equity capital owned either directly or indirectly by non-Japanese

3

Table 1.1 Foreign acquisitions in Japan, 1955–84

Date	Foreign company	Acquired company	Business	Date of acquisition
1955–62	Dow Corning	Fuji Kobunshi	Silicon products (manufacture)	Apr. 1962
1963–6	S. C. Johnson & Sons	Kentoku	Toiletries, wax (manufacture)	Oct. 1966
1967–72	GTE	Kondo Denki Kogyo	Light bulbs for projectors (manufacture)	Apr. 1968
	International Inspection and Testing	Kokusai Kensa	Inspection of machines (service)	Jan. 1970
	Mestra-Holding	Sakura Sokki	Measuring devices (manufacture, sales)	Jun. 1970
	Masten Wright	Nakao Boeki	Insulation materials (trading, sales)	Oct. 1971
	Heidelberger Druckmaschinen	Insatsu Kikai Boeki	Printing machinery (trading, sales)	Nov. 1971
1973–7	BIC	Nakaya Kogyo	Gas lighters, stationery (manufacture)	Nov. 1973
	Grohe Thermostat	Seiwa Shoji	Air conditioning (trading, sales)	Dec. 1974
	Rockaway	Kyoritsu Seiki	Packaging machinery (manufacture)	Sept. 1975
	Ingersoll–Rand	Tokyo Ryuki	Construction machinery (manufacture)	Sept. 1975
	General Motors Acceptance	Isuzu Hanbai Kinyu	Automobile financing (finance)	Jul. 1976
1978–80	Omni Trade	Tatora	Machinery (trading)	Jul. 1978
	Rorer Group	Kyoritsu Yakuhin	Pharmaceuticals (manufacture)	Jul. 1979
	Alcoa	Shibasaki Seisakusho	Bottle caps (manufacture)	Sept. 1979
	Motorola	Aizu Toko	Semiconductors (manufacture)	Oct. 1980
	Clorox	Sanporu	Toiletries, toilet cleaners (manufacture)	Dec. 1980

Table 1.1 (cont)   Foreign acquisitions in Japan, 1955–84

Date	Foreign company	Acquired company	Business	Date of acquisition
1981–4	Boehringer Mannheim	Nikko Bioscience	Medical products, equipment (sales)	Feb. 1981
	Rorer Group	Toho Iyaku	Pharmaceuticals (manufacture)	Mar. 1982
	Groz Beckert	Yoshida Shokai	Sewing machines (sales)	May 1982
	Data General	Nihon Mini Computer	Computers, terminals, software	1st qtr. 1982
	Asean Interest	Sanei Denshi Sangyo	Electronic machinery (manufacture, sales)	3rd qtr. 1982
	Chang Yuan Lung	Sanko Sangyo	Industrial machinery, lubricating oil (export/ import sales)	3rd qtr. 1982
	Kahagan Electronics	Shinnichitoku Denki	Electronic parts (manufacture, sales)	3rd qtr. 1982
	BTR Ltd	Sanshin Kosan	Sundry products (trading)	3rd qtr. 1982
	Merck	Torii Yakuhin	Pharmaceuticals (manufacture, sales)	3rd qtr. 1983
	Merck	Banyu Seiyaku	Pharmaceuticals (manufacture, sales)	3rd qtr. 1983
	Feltex Industries	New Zealand Furniture Japan	Furniture, interior goods (trading, sales)	1st qtr. 1984
	Perkin–Elmer	Nihon Instruments	Semiconductor manufacturing facilities (service)	1st qtr. 1984
	B. Braun Melsungen	Yamamoto Shokai	Medical supplies (trading, sales)	3rd qtr. 1984
	Fersite Corporation	Ueshima Seisakusho	Meters, testers (manufacture, sales)	3rd qtr. 1984
	Cooper Vision	Takada Kikai	Ophthalmic instruments (manufacture, sales)	4th qtr. 1984

Source: Walter Ames, *Harvard International Law Journal*, 1986

Table 1.2 Possible foreign acquisitions (largest minority interest) as of 1984

Foreign company	Japanese company	Business	Ownership (%)
Bayer	Nihon Tokushu Noyaku	Agricultural chemicals (manufacture, trading)	50
Textron	Max	Staples (manufacture)	30
Esso	Toa Menryo	Oil refining	25
Mobil	Toa Menryo	Oil refining	25
Corning International	Iwaki Glass	Glass, ceramics (manufacture)	49.8[a]
Bendix	Akebono Brake	Brakes (manufacture)	19.4
W. L. Gore	Junkoshi	Special electric wires, tubes, films (manufacture)	30
Union Special	Yamamoto Sewing Machine	Industrial sewing machines (manufacture)	35
Citicorp	Fuyo Sogo Lease	Leasing and financing-related industrial facilities	35[b]
General Motors	Isuzu Motors	Automobiles (manufacture)	34.2
Schenk Maschinen	Nagahama Seisakusho	Inspection machines (manufacture)	33.3
Garlock	Arai Seisakusho	Oil seals (manufacture)	22
FMC	Oriental Chain	Chains for machines (manufacture)	25
Alfa Laval	Kyoto Kikai	Dyeing/centrifugal machines (manufacture)	46.5
INCO	Shimura Kako	Nickel products (manufacture)	34.6
George Fisher	Nisshin Koki	Construction machines (manufacture)	33.3
Brunswisk	Sanshin Industries	Motors, auto parts, electric generators (manufacture, sale)	38
Glaxo	Shin Nihon Jitsugyo	Cosmetics, household goods (sale)	50
Nalco Chemical	Hakuto Chemical	Chemical products and medicine (manufacture)	24.8
Chicago Pneumatic Tool	Toku Hambai	Machine tools (wholesale)	50
Moxley	Sony	Consumer electronic products (manufacture)	25
G L Rexroth	Uchida Oil Hydraulics	Oil hydraulic machines (manufacture)	25
Owens Illinois	Nippon Glass	Glass products (manufacture)	40
Eston	Nittan Valve	Automobile valves (manufacture)	12.2

Table 1.2 (cont.) Possible foreign acquisitions (largest minority interest) as of 1984

Foreign company	Japanese company	Business	Ownership (%)
McCormick	Tokai Foods	Spices (manufacture)	49^c
Esso	General Sekiyu	Oil refining	47.4
Simon Container Machinery	Asahi Tekkosho	Paper-making machines (manufacture)	49
Robert Bosch	Diesel Kiki	Auto engines (manufacture)	12.2^d
Swiss Credit Banks	Clarion	Automobile radios (manufacture)	10.4
BOC	Osaka Sanso	Liquid oxygen (manufacture)	24
Thomson CSF	TEAC	Audio equipment (manufacture)	2.8
Showa Shell	Iwata Oil	Oil distribution	40.8
Showa Shell	Nishikawa Oil	Oil distribution	30.7
Luen Sun Investment Co.	Nikkatsu Corp.	Movie distribution	24.5

Notes:
^{a} Asahi Glass Co. also has 49.8% ownership.
^{b} Marubeni Corp. has 33% ownership.
^{c} Lion Dentifrice Co. may have 51%.
^{d} Isuzu Motors has 22.9%.
Source: Walter Ames, *Harvard International Law Journal* , 1986

corporate or individual investors, with individual stakes exceeding US$50,000.

Major Japanese corporations with less than majority foreign ownership, but with non-Japanese corporate or individual investors as their largest shareholders, are listed in Table 1.2.

There are many ways in which foreign investors can do business in Japan. First, it is possible to set up a wholly owned local subsidiary, or to purchase a parcel of land in an industrial park and build a permanent establishment such as a factory. The second way is to enter into an agreement whereby a Japanese corporation receives a license to use a patent or proprietary know-how in exchange for royalty payments. The third method is to set up a Japanese corporation as a joint venture with a local partner or partners. Finally, it *is* possible to acquire an existing Japanese corporation or business.

The first procedure listed above would be ideal for those foreign investors who are interested in industries in which marketing or distribution systems are relatively simple, and open to new entrants with fewer governmental restrictions on production or marketing activities. An example would be the household electrical or electronic appliance industry. This approach is not, however, suitable for industries, such as pharmaceuticals, where the local marketing and distribution systems are very complicated, and where the Japanese government exercises considerable control over production and distribution activities: nor is it suitable where there are practical difficulties in recruiting qualified technical, engineering, production, or marketing personnel.

Then, in a strict sense, simply to give a patent or "know-how" license to a Japanese corporation is far from doing real business in Japan, because foreign licensors are unable to experience the competitiveness of the Japanese market directly.

The third approach is most popular with American and European investors. One of its advantages is that investment costs and risks can be shared with their Japanese partners. On the other hand, there is always the risk of dissolution of the joint venture due to irreconcilable differences of opinion or disputes with Japanese partners over management.

Because of the problems inherent in joint ventures, the fourth way of doing business, acquisition of existing Japanese companies, has recently become increasingly popular with American and European investors. The Rorer Group Inc., a Philadelphia-based pharmaceutical company, is a good example. As shown in Table 1.1, it successfully acquired Kyoritsu Yakuhin Co. Ltd (a Japanese generic house) and Toho Pharmaceutical Laboratory Co. Ltd, and then consolidated the two companies into a new company, Rorer Japan Inc., in December 1984. The president of Rorer Japan is the former owner of the Toho Pharmaceutical Laboratory, while its executive vice-president is the former owner of the Kyoritsu company.

2

Mergers and Acquisitions: Attractive Ways to Enter the Japanese Market

2.1 WHY MERGERS AND ACQUISITIONS HAVE BEEN DISLIKED IN JAPAN

The terms "acquisition" and "purchase of assets" still have unwelcome connotations in Japanese business and legal circles, in which businesses or corporations are not yet generally considered to be subject to sale or purchase. The common understanding of the Japanese Ministry of Justice (MOJ) and the Legal Affairs Bureau (the MOJ department responsible for keeping the Companies Register) seems to be that it would be against the spirit of the law to permit a Japanese corporation to engage in the business of buying and selling other corporations or their assets, either as principal or agent, for commercial purposes; and that therefore, under the laws of Japan, no organization may be set up for the purpose of engaging in such business. In fact, in 1986, when a group of investors tried to form a corporation in Tokyo to (amongst other activities) engage in the brokerage business in connection with mergers and acquisitions, the Tokyo District Legal Affairs Bureau rejected its articles of incorporation on the grounds that they included that purpose. This typical example proves that mergers and acquisitions have not yet been recognized as legitimate commercial transactions in Japan.

Apart from Japanese law itself and the underlying principles of the legal system, for whose benefit do companies exist? Undoubtedly, the majority within Japan would say without hesitation that they exist primarily for the benefit of their employees. Correspondingly, employers and senior business executives are under an obligation to exert their best efforts to assure the financial stability of their employees and, in turn, their dependents.

A Japanese company can be compared to a ship, with the employer and senior executives as its captain and chief officers, and the employees as its crew – a community bound together by a common destiny. For any employee, the corporation for which he works is as important as his own private life, because once he has joined the company he will (under the lifetime employment practice presently prevailing in Japan) spend at least 35–40 years there, probably until he reaches retirement age. As an employee of the company, he experiences the joys and sorrows of life – through human relationships, successes and failures, and promotions and demotions – just as he does at home in his private life. For many Japanese, companies are much more than just the place of work where they are forced to contribute their labor in exchange for a salary and fringe benefits. Therefore attempts by the owner of the company, whether its founder or chief executive officer, to sell the controlling interest to an outsider are seen as a betrayal, analogous to that of the captain of a ship deserting his crew in a storm. Similarly, any person or corporation who attempts to take over or acquire another business or corporation against the will of its current management and/or employees is often considered to be an antisocial challenger of good business morals and practices. Thus the terms "acquisition" and "takeover" have come to be seen as "hijacking" and "extortion."

For more than 2,000 years, the Japanese people subsisted almost exclusively on the fruits of their agricultural labor, sharing their limited crops and enduring the adverse forces of nature shoulder to shoulder. This led to the development of a strong group identity, known as the *mura* or "village community" concept, which requires each of its constituent members not to express his or her freedom of thought or action, but rather to suppress them in order to maintain harmonious and cooperative relations among all members of the group for their improvement as a whole. This is similar to concepts developed in many other agricultural communities. Thus if someone with superior strength or resources tries to reduce such a community or any of its members to submission, he will invariably encounter fierce opposition from the rest of its members. This mentality best manifests itself in the reactions of spectators watching traditional Japanese martial arts such as *sumo*. Most spectators clap and cheer when they see a smaller sumo wrestler defeat a larger opponent. The two most important attitudes of mind, which most Japanese profess to have, can be stated as "it is better to defeat hardness with softness than the other way round" (which is the original fundamental guiding spirit of judo, now popular all over the world) and "sympathy for a tragic hero or gallant loser." Generally, the Japanese like to support the underdog and become extraordinarily resentful when they witness bullying. This can explain why in the Japanese business world, where economics should be the sole guiding principle, any attempt by a person, group, or corporation with large resources to swallow or acquire a corporation with smaller resources – no matter how legitimate the attempt may be according to the law – is often met with great resentment, or even repulsion, sometimes with serious repercussions.

A typical example of how the Japanese might react when a person, who as founder and president of a corporation and having the controlling interest in it, attempts to sell his shares in that corporation to someone else, can be found in the March

3, 1987 issue of the *Nikkei Sangyo Shimbun* newspaper. According to the report, Mr Toshikazu Okuno, who was the president of the Okuno Machinery Works Co. Ltd based in Osaka, one of the leading Japanese manufacturers of equipment for manufacturing springs, announced in February 1987 that he was willing to sell his company at public auction for the minimum price of ¥2 billion. At the time, the company was in a dominant position in the industry, cornering about one-third of the entire Japanese market. Following the announcement, Mr Okuno was approached by more than 20 prospective purchasers, including four foreign companies: they included spring manufacturers, other metal-processing companies, chemical companies, and even a publishing company. Some approached him directly, while others made their bids through securities firms and commercial or investment banks. Quite a few prospective purchasers immediately offered to pay the full asking price in cash. At first, it seemed as though the matter would develop just as it might in the US. However, in Japan, if someone in a rowing boat attempts to do something eccentric, against the will of the other passengers, he will inevitably arouse strong opposition, and his fellow travellers will use all available means to attempt to discourage or dissuade him. Mr Okuno's competitors strongly opposed the proposed sale and asked him to reconsider. As usual, and as expected, their reasoning was that the proposed sale, if it went ahead, would disturb the "established orderly structure of the industry concerned." Their opposition, based on archetypal group consciousness – the common fear of the possible destruction of the boat which they were all aboard – was so strong that Mr Okuno finally abandoned the proposed sale.

Japanese society, particularly the Japanese business community, is more competitive than any other society in the world. Vast numbers of players vie with each other much more intensely than they would with any foreign competitor. In their minds, however, the game must always be played within the same ballpark and in accordance with the same established set of rules. No one is allowed to make up the rules as he goes along!

Thus in Japan, when any person who is the founder, 100% owner, or CEO of a corporation attempts to sell his company, he will encounter very strong socio-psychological business resistance. Naturally, this kind of opposition denounces the idea of selling shares in a business at a profit, by taking the opportunity of its going public, and of using such profit to live a life of luxury or to start a new business. Most founders of corporations or firms hope that they can remain as such for life: if in dire straits due to changes in economic trends or poor management, few of them would resort to selling their companies to overcome the crisis. They would not even consider it. If their businesses were on the verge of bankruptcy, they would continue to make all possible efforts, devoting all their energies to keeping the company afloat, not necessarily for their own benefit but for that of their employees and, in turn, their dependent families. For this reason, Japanese business owners are often criticized for acting as though they were about to commit *harakiri* (ritual suicide by disembowelment). They will not sell their own companies, even if failure to do so results in self-destruction. They will not hesitate to go down with the ship that they captained, if it is about to sink.

Perhaps this explains why, in most past acquisition cases in Japan, the target companies were either bankrupt or nearly bankrupt, and those who acquired them did so rather hesitantly in order to keep them in business – at the request of their owners, major suppliers, and customers. This can be classified as a "rescue from bankruptcy" or "arrangement"-type acquisition. Good examples include the following:

1 *The Riccar Corporation* Riccar was one of the largest manufacturers of sewing machines and other household electrical appliances in Japan. Following its financial collapse, the company filed a petition for reorganization. In 1987, before

15

any court decision was issued on the reorganization plan, the Daiei Corporation, one of the nation's largest supermarket chains, acquired Riccar, which is now expected to be reorganized with Daiei's assistance.

2 *The Heiwa Sogo Bank* The Heiwa Sogo Bank was one of the nation's leading mutual finance banks, based in the Tokyo metropolitan area. In 1986, seriously affected by internal strife amongst its board members and by bad debts on a huge scale arising mostly from unlawful loan transactions, the bank almost folded. The Sumitomo Bank, under the guidance of the Ministry of Finance (MOF), then rescued it from collapse by merging with it, thus saving it from a fate which, in the Japanese economy, must be avoided at all costs.

3 *Osawa & Co* Osawa & Co. Ltd was a medium-sized trading company. Having gone virtually bankrupt, the company filed a petition for reorganization. Its controlling interest was subsequently purchased by the Seibu group of companies, one of the nation's largest marketing groups, to help it comply with the court-approved reorganization plan.

4 *The Sord Corporation* Sord was one of the pioneers of the nation's personal computer industry and was one of the most successful Japanese venture businesses. Following the entry into the personal computer market of large corporations such as NEC, Fujitsu, and IBM, Sord lost its customers to its competitors so rapidly that it almost collapsed in a very short period of time. To save it from bankruptcy, it was subsequently acquired by and became one of the subsidiaries of the Toshiba Corporation.

These examples indicate that successful acquisitions of Japanese corporations need to have several factors in common, if significant opposition from the community or the industry concerned is to be avoided. First, in the above cases the corporations subject to acquisition were bankrupt or nearly bankrupt.

Second, the acquiring parties did not buy them voluntarily for the purpose of pursuing their own interests, but acted rather hesitantly to rescue them and keep them in business, at the request of others. Such acquisitions are very welcome as a legitimate means of guaranteeing jobs for employees and/or to prevent suppliers or subcontractors from going bankrupt as links in a chain reaction – thereby avoiding the unacceptable public image of the strong swallowing the weak.

American and European potential investors would probably regard it as too risky or too unattractive, particularly from the point of view of a potential rate of return, to acquire corporations which are in serious financial difficulties. However, Japanese businessmen, who tend to look at matters on a longer-term basis than their American or European counterparts – often in terms of a decade or two – usually try to see positive merits, even in acquiring corporations that are in such grave financial hardship that they could not expect any return to profitability within 4–5 years (see also Section 4.7).

2.2 AN OPPORTUNE TIME FOR MERGERS AND ACQUISITIONS

Mergers and acquisitions are still considered to be antisocial activities in Japan, as explained in Section 2.1. World business, however, as well as the changing nature of Japan's domestic business, no longer permits the Japanese to confine their economic and industrial activities to traditional behavior patterns. Japanese corporations are not only involved to a certain extent in the mergers and acquisitions boom in the US but, under the currently depressed economic conditions caused by the sharp appreciation of the yen, have also begun to show greater interest than ever in mergers and acquisitions as effective tactics in their struggle for survival through diversification or restructuring. Japanese manufacturers used to recruit new college or university graduates with engineering or science degrees and patiently train them, within their own organizations, into qualified engineers or scientists capable of developing new products, product concepts, or technologies. However, many companies now feel impatient with such conventional time-consuming training and R & D programs.

Along with Japan's newly matured economy, the needs of Japanese consumers are diversifying and changing more rapidly than ever. Many Japanese corporations are beginning to feel that they cannot adequately cope with these rapid changes: they now realize that purchasing R & D capabilities and facilities from outside sources is one of the feasible alternatives that will enable them to achieve necessary changes, and that mergers and acquisitions are a practical approach to accomplishing such purchases. Prompted by these fundamental changes, Japan's economic and industrial society, which has inherited many of the characteristics of the traditional harmonious and tranquil agricultural society, is now entering the age of mergers and acquisitions, a concept originally developed in America and Europe, whose people were traditionally hunters.

As more fully discussed in Chapter 7, the only available statistical information on the number of mergers and acquisitions in Japan is that published by the Fair Trade Commission (FTC). This information has been compiled by the FTC on the basis of papers filed under the statutory filing system that it administers. Under Section 15.2 of the Antimonopoly Act, as amended, every Japanese corporation is required, when it amalgamates or merges or is amalgamated or merged with any other corporation or corporations, to file an application with the FTC at least 30 days prior to the proposed effective date of the amalgamation or merger. By virtue of Section 16 of the Act, the same requirement also applies to every corporation acquiring all, or substantially all, of the assets located in Japan of any other corporation. It should be noted that the foregoing statutory filing requirement applies only to mergers, amalgamations, and acquisitions of assets. It does not apply to acquisitions of corporations through the purchase of shares or equitable interests. Needless to say, in Japan the acquisition of a corporation through the purchase of its shares or equitable interests is as important a form of acquisition as it is in the US. Therefore it should be noted that, as far as acquisitions are concerned, the official statistical data given below are very restricted.

The data show that the number of mergers has been on the increase since 1980. The same applies to the number of cases involving the acquisition of assets. Combined, the numbers hit a historical peak in 1985 (see Figure 2.1 and Table 2.1). FTC analysts predict that the number of mergers, acquisitions, and assets transfers will continue to increase during the years to come, particularly in those industries which have been most adversely affected by the further internationalization of the Japanese economy and/or the sharp appreciation of the yen against the currencies of her major trading partners, and which are eagerly seeking to restructure themselves within the present-day world economy.

Apart from the statistical data, how do top Japanese business executives feel about mergers and acquisitions? Numerous opinion polls have been conducted over the past couple of years in order to determine changing attitudes towards mergers and acquisitions.

In July 1985, Yamaichi Securities Co. Ltd, one of the nation's leading securities firms, sent a questionnaire entitled "Strategies for mergers, acquisitions and other forms of business cooperation" to 7,225 corporations throughout the country, and obtained 587 replies.

When asked, "Would you use merger or acquisition as part of your operational strategy?," 56.4% of those who replied answered "Yes," while 40% answered "No." When further asked, "Do you have in mind any particular corporation, firm or business which you would like to acquire immediately, if available?," 13% answered "Yes," and 81.3% "No." When

Table 2.1 The annual numbers of merger and acquisition cases filed with the FTC, 1947–85

Year	Number of mergers	Number of assets acquisitions	Annual totals
1947	23	22	45
1948	309	192	501
1949	571	196	767
1950	420	209	629
1951	331	182	513
1952	385	124	509
1953	344	126	470
1954	325	167	492
1955	338	143	481
1956	381	209	590
1957	398	140	538
1958	381	118	499
1959	413	139	552
1960	440	144	584
1961	591	162	753
1962	715	193	908
1963	997	223	1,220
1964	864	195	1,059
1965	894	202	1,096
1966	871	264	1,135
1967	995	301	1,296
1968	1,020	354	1,374
1969	1,163	391	1,554
1970	1,147	413	1,560
1971	1,178	449	1,627
1972	1,184	452	1,636
1973	1,028	443	1,471
1974	995	420	1,415
1975	957	429	1,386
1976	941	511	1,452
1977	1,011	646	1,657
1978	898	595	1,493
1979	871	611	1,482
1980	961	680	1,641
1981	1,044	771	1,815
1982	1,040	815	1,855
1983	1,020	702	1,722
1984	1,096	790	1,886
1985	1,113	807	1,920

Note: before June 18, 1949 earlier legislation, under which mergers and acquisitions were subject to prior governmental approval, was in effect. The present legislation has been in effect since that date.
Source: FTC Report No. 761/1986

Attractive Ways to Enter the Japanese Market

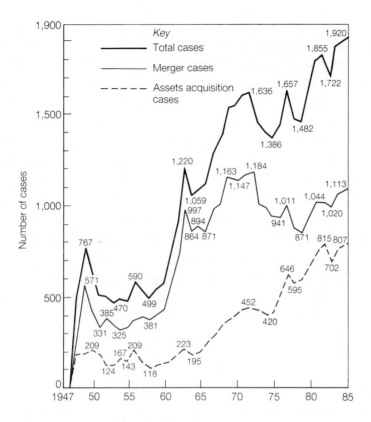

Figure 2.1 The number of merger and acquisition cases filed with the FTC, 1947–85. Before June 18, 1949 earlier legislation, under which mergers and acquisitions were subject to prior governmental approval, was in effect. The present legislation has been in effect since that date.
Source: FTC Report No. 761/1986.

asked, "From whom would you seek advice if your corporation were to merge with or acquire any other corporation or the assets of any other corporation?," 36.4% replied that they would seek advice from their bankers, 24.3% from certified public accountants or tax consultants, and 25.2% from their lawyers: notably, only 3.5% said that they would contact securities firms – the Japanese equivalent of investment banks in the US. As to the purpose of mergers, acquisitions, or purchases of assets, 34.3% answered "for diversification," 29.0% "for the expansion of the company's base of operations," 21.8% "to supplement corporate resources such as technologies, human resources, production and/or R & D facilities and know-how," and 10.6% "for the furtherance of rationalization or restructuring." When further asked, "Would you use the services of finders or brokers for mergers or acquisitions?," 63.9% of those who replied said that they would do so, even for a fee, 19.7% answered that they would *not* do so, even free of charge, while 10.9% simply said that they would not pay for such services. This is very interesting when contrasted with the US, where corporations are obliged to pay for such services. In reply to the same question in respect of mergers and acquisitions overseas, 5.5% said that they would be prepared to pay. To the question, "Do you expect mergers and acquisitions to become increasingly popular in Japan?," 83.3% replied positively. These results support the view that mergers and acquisitions will become increasingly popular in Japan, and thus will increasingly be used as a method of achieving strategic operational objectives.

In a second 1985 survey, Nomura Securities Co. Ltd (one of the world's largest securities companies) sent questionnaires to 8,859 corporations (including 1,808 listed corporations) and received 927 replies. Approximately 75% of the respondents were very interested in mergers and acquisitions, including 19.8% who considered mergers and acquisitions as an important method of achieving their strategic operational objectives (23.9% expressed specific interest). When asked, "What particular objectives would you hope to achieve by merger or acquisition?," 47.1% wished "to strengthen research and development capabilities," 37.9% aimed "for diversification," 27.1% "for the expansion of sales outlets," and 27.1% "for the expansion of the company's operational base related or conducive to existing operations." While these results reveal the increasing level of interest, foreign corporations are not necessarily seen as potential targets. According to the Nomura poll, 55.8% of respondents said that they would consider only Japanese corporations as potential merger or acquisition targets, while only half that number (29%) said that they would not hesitate to merge with or acquire foreign corporations. At the very least, the traditional psychological aversion seems to have begun to disappear.

Following these two polls, Shoji Homu Kenkyukai, a non-profit-making research and publishing organization specializing in commercial law, conducted a very specific survey on mergers and acquisitions in December 1985. Questionnaires were mailed to 6,689 corporations (including 1,968 listed corporations); 33% of the listed corporations and approximately 8% of the nonlisted corporations replied. The results highlighted the gulf between what the Japanese commonly say and what they actually intend to do. Despite the strong interest which they expressed in mergers and acquisitions, most of the influential businessmen showed remarkable timidity or naivety when asked what tactics they would actually employ.

When asked, "What percentage of shares would you purchase in a target company, if you were to acquire it?," 45.9% replied "at least 50%," while 30.2% said "it would depend on the circumstances of each case," 8.7% opted for "100%," and 3.5% "at least 20%." At first glance, this seems to indicate that most Japanese corporations would not just acquire another corporation for portfolio investment purposes but would go as far as acquiring the controlling interest. However, their answers to a second question varied quite considerably. When asked "Would you hesitate to resort to tender offer – TOB under Section 27-II of the Securities and Exchange Act, as amended – if you were to attempt to acquire a majority interest in any other corporation?," 79.7% of respondents said that they would, while only 8.7% said they would not, if they could obtain the consent of the management of the target corporation. None of the respondents said that they would resort to tender offer with or without such consent. Further, when asked, "What would you do, if you were in a situation where you were acquiring or wanted to acquire a majority interest in another corporation and you had no means available other than tender offer to accomplish the acquisition?," 80% were still adamant that they would not use tender offer. This amounts to an admission that, in such an eventuality, they would abandon the proposed acquisition completely. In short, this poll revealed that most Japanese corporations are still very negative or skeptical about uninvited, hostile, or potentially hostile tender offers or acquisitions, for a variety of reasons. According to 34.3% of respondents, since Japanese corporations had few floating stockholders, a tender offer would not be effective; 32.0% considered that a tender offer would damage their reputation; 30.8% that a tender offer would trigger a hike in the share price of the target corporation and would inevitably make acquisition costly; 30.2% felt that a tender offer would work against their interests because it would stir up opposition or hostility among the employees of the target corporation; and 12.2% that it would arouse opposition or hostility among the banks and other financial institutions dealing with the target corporation. Surprisingly, as many as 11.0% expressed fears about maintaining confidentiality: during the 10-day statutory prior notice requirement period in Japan – quite unlike US practice – an unauthorized leakage of information might reveal the proposed tender offer to outsiders and eventually spoil the entire acquisition scheme, or cause other problems such as a sudden rise in the price of the target corporation's stock. It is difficult to estimate a specific percentage, since the participants in this poll were allowed to give two or more answers to each question, but it is probably safe to say that most respondents were very negative about tender offers because they feared damage to their reputation and/or opposition or hostility from others, including the employees of the target company.

Thus even most of those senior Japanese businessmen who consider that in acquiring another corporation they must gain the controlling equitable interest still believe that tender offers, even if successful, would do more harm than good. They firmly believe that in Japan the successful management and operation of a corporation, whatever its role in a merger or acquisition, depend very much on its reputation in the business community, particularly amongst its suppliers, customers, bankers, and competitors.

In the Shoji Homu Kenkyukai poll participants were specifically asked, "What measures or tactics have you introduced or employed to defeat, prevent or discourage hostile or uninvited acquisitions? If you have not already introduced or employed such measures or tactics, what measures or tactics would you introduce or employ, if your corporation became or were threatened with becoming a target of a hostile or uninvited acquisition?" – questions of great interest to foreign companies which hope to make Japanese acquisitions. The most popular measure was to encourage and retain as many loyal major shareholders as possible. Again it is dangerous to draw any definite conclusions because of the multiplicity of answers. However, 49.6% answered that they had employed or would employ this measure to discourage a hostile or uninvited acquisition; 35.4% replied that they would keep a close watch on changes in share ownership; 18% would closely monitor share transactions with the assistance of their main underwriters; 16.5% said that they already had inserted – or would in future insert – a clause in their articles of incorporation restricting the right to transfer shares (this will be discussed in more detail below); and 10.2% stated that they would ask their main banks for assistance.

The main underwriter system is unique to Japan, as is the main bank system. All listed and most major unlisted corporations have at least one of the leading securities firms as their main or managing underwriter, just as each has its respective main bank. The bank which has the closest or longest business relationship with a corporation – often the one most involved with loan finance – is known as its main bank. The main or managing underwriter is a leading securities firm which acts as the corporation's chief financial adviser and as its manager in underwriting or distributing the issue of equity or debt securities – no mere stockbroker or commission agent is entitled to act as the "main underwriter."

Legally permissible restriction of the ability to transfer shares is considered to be one of the most practical ways of discouraging hostile or uninvited acquisition. Under the provisions of the Commercial Code (as amended), stock corporations, other than those whose shares are listed or traded on any stock exchange or over-the-counter market, are permitted to have in the articles of incorporation a clause to the effect that any transfer of their shares shall be subject to the approval of the board of directors, thereby effectively preventing any person who is not reasonably acceptable to the board of directors from becoming a shareholder. For such a provision to be effective, it must be inserted in the articles of incorporation and be registered with the Companies Register.

Potential foreign investors may be surprised to learn that as many as 336 corporations (32.9% of the respondents) answered that they had taken no measures at all to discourage acquisition attempts; primarily because virtually no Japanese corporation has ever become the target of a hostile or uninvited acquisition. In a sense, this situation is of course favorable to foreign investors. The various legal obstacles that currently exist in the relevant statutes are another reason for Japanese indifference toward such measures. In the questionnaire, respondents were quizzed about their knowledge of the legal obstacles which prevent them from employing defeating, preventive, or discouraging measures (potential foreign investors need to be well versed in these obstacles, which will be discussed in more detail later). Section 211-II of the Commercial Code (as amended), which generally prohibits any corporation from purchasing shares in its parent corporation, was most frequently pointed out:

Section 211-II No corporation (hereinafter referred to as "Subsidiary Corporation") shall be permitted to acquire shares in any corporation holding a majority of its issued and outstanding shares (hereinafter referred to as "Parent Corporation") . . . , unless (i) such acquisition is made as part of a merger transaction or of the acquisition of all of the assets of any other corporation; or (ii) such acquisition is necessary to enable the Subsidiary Corporation, in the exercise of any right to which it is entitled, to accomplish any purpose or purposes for which such exercise is made.

Thus no corporation is legally permitted to acquire shares in any other corporation, if a majority of its issued and outstanding shares is owned by the other corporation; nor is it legally possible for a Japanese subsidiary corporation to acquire shares in the parent corporation in an attempt to prevent the latter's hostile or uninvited acquisitions.

The next major legal obstacle that Japanese corporations face in employing preventative measures is the statutory restriction imposed by Section 241.3 of the Code on cross stock ownership:

Section 241.3 No stock corporation or proprietary corporation shall be entitled to exercise any voting rights which it would otherwise be entitled to exercise on any share or shares of any other corporation, if more than a quarter of its issued and outstanding shares is owned by such other corporation alone or if such other corporation is the Parent Corporation of any third corporation or corporations which alone or jointly with its or their Parent Corporation own more than a quarter of the issued and outstanding shares of the first mentioned corporation.

Thus Section 241.3 prohibits any corporation from exercising voting rights on its shares in any other corporation, if more than 25% of its share issue is owned by that other corporation. Also, if any two corporations each own more than 25% of the issued and outstanding shares of the other, neither shall be entitled to exercise voting rights on its shares in the other. The same restriction also applies to shares of any corporation X owned by any other corporation Y, if Y is the parent corporation of any third corporation or corporations Z which, alone or jointly with corporation Y, own more than 25% of the issued and outstanding shares of corporation X. The denial of voting rights under this provision functions as an indirect obstacle to the use, by Japanese corporations of cross stock ownership, of preventive measures to discourage acquisitions.

In addition, Section 210 of the Code generally prohibits corporations from acquiring their own shares:

Section 210 No corporation shall be permitted to acquire its own shares, unless (i) they are acquired for cancellation; (ii) they are acquired as part of a merger transaction or of the acquisition of all of the assets of any other corporation; or (iii) their acquisition is necessary to enable it, in the exercise of any right to which it is entitled, to accomplish any purpose or purposes for which such exercise is made, nor shall it be permitted to accept its own shares in excess of one-twentieth of its then issued and outstanding shares as a pledge.

Furthermore, Section 241 of the Code prohibits corporations from exercising voting rights on any of its own shares which it holds in its treasury.

Thus while corporations in the US are allowed to acquire and own their own capital stock shares as treasury stock, under the Commercial Code Japanese corporations are generally prohibited at all times from acquiring or owning their own capital stock shares. Because of this, they are unable to purchase their own shares on the market through "self-tender offer" as a means of preventing an acquisition or tender offer by others.

The Antimonopoly Act (as amended) is another piece of legislation which provides similar obstacles. Section 11 of the Act prohibits "financial institutions" from acquiring or holding the shares of any other corporation in excess of a certain limit:

Section 11 No corporation engaged in the financial business shall acquire or hold shares in any other corporation in Japan in excess of 5% (or 10% if such corporation is engaged in the insurance business . . .) of the issued and outstanding shares of such other corporation . . .

Furthermore, Section 9 of the Act makes the following provisions:

Section 9.1 No holding company may be established.

Section 9.2 No corporation, whether domestic or foreign, shall become or act as a holding company in Japan.

Section 9.3 The term "holding company" as used in Sections 9.1 and 9.2 shall mean a corporation whose primary business is to control the operations of any other corporation or corporations in Japan through stock or equity ownership.

Thus in Japan holding companies cannot exist as they do in the US. Under the Act as it now stands, no Japanese corporation may have any one of its banks hold more than 5% of its shares, whether or not to prevent an uninvited acquisition, although each bank may hold up to 5% of the shares. Nor may a Japanese corporation be directly or indirectly involved in the setting up of a holding company that can then hold its shares to prevent an uninvited acquisition, as American corporations frequently do.

In 1987, a campaign was jointly launched by the Federation of Economic Organizations (the nation's largest association of business executives) and the Liberal Democratic Party (a conservative political party with a majority in both Houses of the Diet, which has been in power for over 40 years) to reform the Antimonopoly Act. The main objective of the movement is to promote new legislation to abolish Section 9-II of the Act, which reads as follows:

Section 9-II No stock corporation having share capital . . . of ¥10 billion or more or a net assets value . . . of ¥30 billion or more, other

29

than a corporation engaged in the financial business, . . . shall be permitted to acquire or hold shares in any other corporation or corporations in Japan in excess of, based on their acquisition cost . . ., the amount of its share capital or its net assets value, whichever is the greater . . .

Obviously, the main impetus behind the campaign is the dissatisfaction of large Japanese businesses with their inability to use subsidiaries freely as tools in achieving strategic operational objectives. However, their real objective in launching the campaign is, on the one hand, to promote new legislation which would allow Japanese corporations to organize holding companies – so that mergers, acquisitions, divestiture, or other restructuring could be carried out more easily – and, on the other hand, create the opportunity to review and hopefully remove the statutory obstacles that now exist under the Antimonopoly Act and the Commercial Code, so that groups of companies could be organized that would be in a better position to compete internationally.

2.3 RECENT ACQUISITIONS OF JAPANESE COMPANIES BY WESTERN CORPORATIONS

One noteworthy aspect of recent cases of acquisition of Japanese companies by American and European corporations is that a significant number of these acquisitions were of Japanese pharmaceutical companies. This might be partly due to the fact that the existing governmental control over the retail price of most prescription items has had a significantly adverse effect on the profitability of some of the domestic pharmaceutical companies, making them relatively easy to acquire. It may also be partly attributed to the complexity of the distribution system of pharmaceutical products in Japan, and to the governmental control over their manufacture, import, and distribution. These controls have created a climate in which American and European potential investors in the Japanese pharmaceutical and medical supply industries feel that it is easier to acquire existing Japanese firms than to establish new operations of their own in Japan.

For example, Merck & Co. Inc. successfully acquired the Torii Pharmaceutical Co. Ltd in 1983 and then the Banyu Pharmaceutical Co. Ltd in the same year, both through friendly takeovers. In the case of Banyu Pharmaceutical, at a meeting held on August 3, 1983, Banyu's board of directors decided to issue 74 million additional common shares and US dollar denominated bonds, which were convertible into 40 million common shares, and to allot these additional shares and convertible bonds exclusively to Merck. (Allotment of additional shares or other securities to a particular person or persons, known as *daisansha wariate* in Japan, as a means of accomplishing friendly takeovers, will be discussed in more detail later.) As a result of this allotment, together with the acquisition of 6.07 million Banyu Pharmaceutical common shares in March 1982, Merck has acquired 50.02% of the Banyu common shares. As Banyu Pharmaceutical's president reported at a press conference at the time:

We received an acquisition offer from Merck some time after March 1982, and were told that Merck's primary interest in acquiring Banyu was to develop Banyu as an internationally competitive pharmaceutical manufacturing company in Japan. We, at the management of Banyu, thought that becoming a member of the Merck Group at a time when Banyu's operation and performance were in a relatively stable condition would provide Banyu with a good opportunity to strengthen its operational foundation upon which our future growth could be based. Since Banyu and Merck have trusted each other through friendly business relations which have lasted for over 30 years, we have no concern whatsoever about giving Merck controlling interest in Banyu. The two companies have agreed that the present management of Banyu will continue to manage and operate

Banyu as before, that Banyu will continue with the Japanese-style personnel administration and labor management practices as before, allowing its employees to participate in the management of the company and giving them fair opportunity for promotion as before, and that it will continue to carry out its business substantially in the same manner as before paying due respect to the traditions of and the business customs and practices prevailing in the Japanese pharmaceutical industry.

By referring to over 30 years of amicable business ties between the two companies, he primarily meant Nippon Merck Banyu Co. Ltd, which had been set up as a joint venture, owned equally by Merck and Banyu, over three decades ago (however, share ownership in Nippon Merck Banyu had subsequently changed to 50.5% Merck and 49.5% Banyu). It is said that Merck invested some ¥80 billion and ¥4 billion to acquire Banyu and Torii respectively (see also Section 4.4).

Other examples of acquisitions of Japanese pharmaceutical firms by American and European investors include: the two acquisitions by the Rorer Group of Kyoritsu Yakuhin and the Toho Pharmaceutical Laboratory, which took place in 1979 and 1982 respectively (already referred to in Chapter 1); the equity participation by Merrell Dow Corporation, one of Dow Chemical's subsidiaries, in the Funai Pharmaceutical Co. Ltd (March 1985) and its subsequent purchase of Funai's additional common shares, increasing its holdings in Funai up to 57.6% (March 1986); and Nippon Boehringer Mannheim's 1986 acquisition of 100% of San'a Pharmaceutical, a relatively new manufacturer with 110 employees and an annual sales revenue of ¥4.2 billion. San'a was in financial trouble at the time and was looking for assistance from a resourceful foreign firm.

According to a newspaper report, on July 18, 1985 Siemens, the giant German firm, acquired Sagami Denki Co. Ltd, a Tokyo-based manufacturer of hearing aids with a share capital of ¥17.5 million, which was in financial trouble at the time.

Adolf Würth, a manufacturer of high-quality tools and industrial fasteners, primarily for automotive use, based in Baden Wurttemberg, West Germany, was looking for an opportunity to open and maintain a sales outlet in Japan. In 1986 it appointed the Keiyo Screw Co. Ltd, an industrial fastener manufacturer located in Chiba Prefecture, with a share capital of ¥4 million, as distributor of its products in Japan. This arrangement was so successful that it became very interested in having equity participation in Keiyo. In July 1987, Würth announced the acquisition of two-thirds of the outstanding Keiyo common shares. This acquisition was accomplished by allotment to and purchase by Adolf Würth of 16,000 additional Keiyo common shares for some ¥100 million. Würth already owned 8,000 Keiyo common shares prior to this purchase, and therefore became Keiyo's largest shareholder, with 66.7% of the outstanding common voting shares.

There have been a few cases in which founders and owners of successful Japanese companies have sold their firms to American or European corporations because they had no sons or daughters to whom they could hand over the business. One typical example is that of Tokyo Kaken, a small but very profitable company with over 40 employees and an annual sales revenue of ¥500 million. Its founder and owner had retired and handed his company down to his son, but soon thereafter the son died suddenly. Therefore the father, who was over 80 years of age at the time, was forced to take on the management of the company again. On account of his age and the fact that he could not find a suitable successor, he finally decided to sell. However, he then faced a problem. If it became public knowledge that he was going to sell, it might give rise to an erroneous rumor that the company was in financial trouble – and such speculation could have a serious adverse effect on the company's business. Consequently, he finally decided to sell the company to an American or European corporation wishing to do business in Japan, in the belief that – from the point of view of confidentiality – this would be a safer course of action. He approached a friend who was a member of the Diet to seek his help and advice, and was introduced to Rawpack Corporation, a California-based manufacturer of plastic packaging. Rawpack, which was a middle-sized company with seven factories in North America and an annual sales revenue of ¥7.0 billion, was attempting to enter the Japanese market, and so the timing was very good for both parties. It did not take long for them to negotiate and enter into a formal purchase agreement, under which the owner sold his entire company to Rawpack as a going concern.

There have also been a significant number of cases reported recently in which American and European manufacturers have acquired a substantial percentage of equity ownership in their Japanese distributors: prominent amongst these are the cases of Electrolux and Martini Rossi. In the former instance, in June 1986 Electrolux Japan Co. Ltd, a wholly owned Tokyo subsidiary (with a paid-up share capital of ¥450 million) of the Electrolux Corporation (the Swedish manufacturer of electrical and electronic appliances), acquired substantially all of the business and assets of Bokusui Kosan Co. Ltd, a Tokyo-based company with a paid-up share capital of ¥90 million, which was acting as the exclusive distributor of Electrolux products in Japan. In the latter case, in July 1986 Martini Rossi S.p.A., the wine and spirits producer based in Turin, Italy, acquired a 65% stake in the Nichiou Trading Co. Ltd, a Tokyo-based firm which was then acting as the distributor of Martini Rossi products in Japan.

A few cases have also been reported lately in which American and European corporations have acquired foreign-capital-based Japanese corporations. One typical example is the Prudential/Simmons case. The Prudential Asia Investment Corporation, an American investment company, acquired Simmons Japan Co. Ltd through leveraged buy-out. Simmons Japan was a subsidiary of the US-based Simmons Corporation, a manufacturer and distributor of high-quality beds. This was the first leveraged buy-out in Japan, and therefore it attracted considerable media interest.

2.4 RECENT ACQUISITIONS OF JAPANESE COMPANIES BY JAPANESE CORPORATIONS

As mentioned earlier, there have recently been an increasing number of cases in which Japanese corporations have acquired other Japanese corporations. Also, there has been a general increase in the number of business executives who have attempted to use acquisition as a method of strengthening the operational base of the groups under their command. In this section, a post-mortem will be conducted on several acquisition cases involving Japanese corporations only, in order to assist American or European potential purchasers in gaining a better understanding of how things happen in Japan.

2.4.1 *Minebea* vs. *Sankyo Seiki*: An attempted hostile acquisition

It is generally alleged that hostile acquisitions, which are commonplace in the US, have never been attempted, successfully or otherwise, in Japan. However, this is not so. In fact, the legal practice to which the author belongs has had experience in, and is presently working on, several American-style hostile acquisition cases. In addition, among past cases which were publicly reported as being friendly acquisitions, more than a few began as hostile acquisition attempts, and only became "amicable" after desperate struggles between the parties concerned. Without doubt, the case of hostile acquisition which has been most conspicuously featured in the newspapers is that of *Minebea* vs. *Sankyo Seiki* – an attempt which eventually failed completely.

The facts, as reconstructed on the basis of relevant newspaper reports, are as follows.

At a press conference held at the Tokyo Stock Exchange on August 15, 1985, Minebea Co. Ltd, which is the world's largest manufacturer of miniature bearings and is well known for its aggressive acquisition tactics, and for certain successful acquisitions made not only in Japan but also in America and Europe, announced that it was making a hostile acquisition attempt: the target company was to be Sankyo Seiki, a Nagano-based company which was the world's largest manufacturer of music boxes and which also manufactured electrical and electronic components.

Minebea had begun to purchase the common shares of Sankyo Seiki in 1984, about a year previously. It had purchased them on the open market in a number of small transactions through as many as ten different brokers, so as not to stimulate the market price of Sankyo Seiki stock to its own disadvantage and to prevent Sankyo Seiki from becoming aware of its intentions. In parallel with those purchases, Minebea also bought a substantial amount of convertible bonds which Sankyo Seiki had previously issued on overseas capital markets by private placement. By the end of 1985, it had purchased at least 14,100,000 common shares in Sankyo Seiki, including some 5 million shares acquired upon conversion of the convertible bonds. This holding represented 19.1% of the then issued and outstanding common shares of Sankyo Seiki, and so Minebea became Sankyo Seiki's largest shareholder. It is believed that the convertible bonds were purchased directly from their owners, mostly foreign investment or commercial banks, rather than on the open market.

Since many Japanese corporations have issued convertible bonds on overseas capital markets, purchasing outstanding bonds is now considered to be one of the practical ways of amassing the common shares of Japanese corporations. One of the advantages of purchasing these convertible bonds is that, unlike common shares, they can be purchased *en bloc* on a confidential basis directly from their owners who, in most cases, are American or European investment or commercial banks. Alternatively, they can be purchased quietly on the open market, in substantial numbers, without provoking a price hike. In addition to Minebea, there are several other well-known instances in which investors have purchased convertible bonds issued by Japanese corporations in bulk on secondary markets. One such case involves a certain investment company based in the UK which hit the headlines with its purchase of a substantial number of convertible bonds issued by Tokyo Sanyo Electric and its purchase on secondary markets of a substantial number of those issued by the Fujita Tourist Company on foreign capital markets, taking advantage of an attempt by a certain Japanese arbitrageur to purchase and amass a large number of Fujita Tourist's common shares on the Japanese stock market.

From its vantage point as the largest shareholder, with 19.1% of the issued and outstanding common shares of Sankyo Seiki, Minebea formally proposed to Sankyo Seiki that they should merge. The proposed merger was, however, rejected by the management of Sankyo Seiki, which then went on to explain that they had become aware of Minebea's purchases of its shares as early as the end of 1984, on the basis of information provided by its managing underwriter, Nikko Securities. As soon as they had become aware of Minebea's intentions, they had launched a secret program, with the assistance of Nikko Securities, to increase the number of loyal and stable stockholders. They had successfully persuaded their banks (including the Hachijuni Bank, which was and still is their main bank), other financial institutions, including life and nonlife insurance companies, and their major suppliers and customers to buy and hold their shares. In turn, the Hachijuni Bank had apparently persuaded the Taiyo Kobe Bank and the Mitsubishi Bank to purchase and agree to hold an additional 500,000 to 1 million shares of Sankyo Seiki's common stock. As a result, the percentage of shares held by shareholders who were loyal to Sankyo Seiki increased from 52% to approximately 55% of its then issued and outstanding common shares by late 1985 or early 1986.

When it became conscious of this strategy, Minebea announced that it was "in no hurry to proceed with its negotiations" with Sankyo Seiki, and that although it was not presently considering making a tender offer to increase its holding of Sankyo Seiki stock, it was making the necessary arrangements to enable it to obtain additional financing in the form of a syndicated loan or loans just in case it did make a tender offer. This announcement attracted the keen attention of the Japanese press, which immediately began to speculate that the matter might eventually develop into the first hostile takeover bid in Japan. However, it did not.

Sankyo Seiki allegedly succeeded in further increasing the numbers and holdings of its loyal shareholders very rapidly, with more than 10 million additional shares being bought and held by its banks, other financial institutions, and its major suppliers and customers: this included some 500,000–800,000 additional shares each bought and held by the Hachijuni Bank and the Long-Term Credit Bank of Japan, as well as 6.3 million additional shares bought and held by its other banks, including the Mitsubishi Bank, the Industrial Bank of Japan, and the Taiyo Kobe Bank. This action, coupled with announcements by the Mitsubishi Bank and the Industrial Bank of Japan that they would acquire additional Sankyo Seiki common shares in the future if necessary, finally scuppered Minebea's attempted merger.

The way in which Sankyo Seiki was so successful in defeating Minebea's scheme within a relatively short period of time was amazing. The most important factor was the assistance from its banks, one of the tangible benefits of Japan's unique main bank system. The main bank of a corporation, particularly one that is listed, is usually not only the largest lender to that corporation, but also one of its major shareholders, holding its common shares within the limit set out by the Antimonopoly Act (as amended). As far as the corporation is concerned, it is a loyal and stable shareholder. A main bank would not part with its shares in a corporation against the will of the corporation's management as long as it held that privileged position, unless the corporation was on the verge of bankruptcy. If a main bank were to venture to part with its shares in a corporation in order to seek a capital gain by taking advantage of an acquisition attempt, the bank would not only immediately lose the confidence of the corporation, but would also quickly ruin its general reputation. And since the banking business is totally dependent on public confidence, it could prove fatal for any bank to run such a risk.

After the failure of the merger attempt, Minebea stopped buying additional shares in Sankyo. Instead, it launched a psychological campaign against Sankyo Seiki's management, sending them a letter of enquiry in February 1986 asking about their management and operational policies, and another in May 1986 again recommending a merger. Those letters were followed by a derivative suit. On July 31, 1987, on behalf of Sankyo Seiki and all its shareholders, Minebea instituted a derivative suit against three members of the Sankyo Seiki board of directors, including Mr Rokuichi Yamada, its president, seeking an award for damages in the amount of ¥370 million to compensate for the damage allegedly sustained by Sankyo Seiki as a result of "being authorized and caused by the defendants to purchase its own shares in violation of the statutory ban under the Commercial Code, as amended." The complaint alleged the following: that the defendants illegally authorized and caused certain subsidiaries of Sankyo Seiki, which were Sankyo Seiki's *alter egos*, to purchase approximately 1,360,000 Sankyo Seiki common shares; that they caused the subsidiaries to sell all but 10,000 of these shares below cost, thereby causing the subsidiaries, and consequently the Sankyo Seiki parent company,

damage in the amount mentioned above; and that the defendants were liable, jointly and severally, to compensate Sankyo
Seiki for this damage. It was reported that the real intention was
to harass Sankyo Seiki's top executives and force them to the
negotiating table. However, further opposition on the part of
Sankyo Seiki apparently confounded this tactic, and stalemate
persisted until March 25, 1988.

On that date, the business world was shocked by a report that
Minebea had sold its entire holding of 14,100,000 Sankyo Seiki
shares of common stock to the Tokyo Pigeon Co. Ltd, one of
Sankyo Seiki's subsidiaries, thereby abandoning the acquisition
attempt completely. According to the report, Minebea sold the
shares at ¥1,100 per share, way below the average purchase
price of ¥1,380 per share, and thus suffered a huge capital loss
of almost ¥4 billion.

The person who acted as the intermediary between Minebea
and Sankyo Seiki, and who wrote the retreating scenario for
Minebea, was Mr Mitsuo Goto, the executive managing director
of JAFCO, Japan's largest venture capital company, which was
a member of the Nomura Securities group.

Before he joined JAFCO, Mr Goto had been an executive
officer of Nomura Securities. Consequently, he took action
immediately by meeting Mr Takami Takahashi, chairman of the
Minebea board of directors, on February 20, 1988 and obtained
his authorization to represent Minebea in selling the 14,100,000
shares. With this sanction, he contacted Mr Takezo Yokouchi,
who still wielded great influence over Sankyo Seiki as a special
adviser, on February 27 and subsequently reached agreement
with Sankyo to arrange the repurchase of Minebea's shares on
March 1.

However, this was not the end of the episode. In fact it was
only the beginning of one of the nation's largest acquisition
events since World War II, involving two major companies,
both of which are listed on the First Section of the Tokyo Stock
Exchange.

On July 29, 1988, Sankyo Seiki and Nippon Steel Corporation (NSC), the world's largest steel manufacturing company, jointly announced that NSC would purchase all of Sankyo's 14,100,000 shares of common stock which the Sankyo Seiki group had repurchased from Minebea in March, and enter into a full-scale business cooperation arrangement with Sankyo Seiki.

By this undertaking, NSC became Sankyo's largest shareholder and virtually acquired the company – which had chosen NSC rather than Minebea as its parent company. NSC acted as a "white knight," although somewhat belatedly: and the person who was reported to have successfully persuaded NSC to act was Mr Kazuo Ibuki, chairman of the Mitsubishi Bank, Sankyo's main bank. Mr Ibuki had been acquainted with Sankyo Seiki's management when he was manager of the Mitsubishi Bank's branch in Shimbashi, Tokyo, where Sankyo Seiki's Tokyo head office was originally located. At Sankyo's request, secret deals were arranged in close cooperation with the Hachijuni Bank, a commercial bank based in Nagano, where Sankyo Seiki's headquarters was located. Mr Ibuki met NSC's chairman, Mr Yutaka Takeda, who in turn was a close colleague of Mr Masahiko Yamada, the honorary chairman of Sankyo Seiki, through their membership of a business association, and learned that NSC was extremely interested in purchasing the shares.

Further negotiations then culminated in NSC's acquisition of Sankyo Seiki: "Nippon Steel," said Mr Yamada, "is a gentlemanly company that we can fully depend on and have complete confidence in."

NSC paid slightly over ¥15.3 billion (¥1,088 per share) for the 14,100,000 shares and gained two seats on Sankyo's board of directors. "We will be satisfied," said one of NSC's senior officials, "if one of the members of Sankyo Seiki's board appointed by us is made a senior executive director. We assure you we are not seeking the part of president" (see also Sections 5.7.2 and 5.9).

41

Before its unsuccessful attempt to merge with Sankyo Seiki, Minebea had made an unsuccessful merger proposal to another listed company in the early 1970s: at that time, the target was Tokyo Keiki Co. Ltd, a leading manufacturer of aviation and navigation instruments and hydraulic equipment, based in Tokyo. Minebea, which at the time was the second largest shareholder of Tokyo Keiki, owning 10 million shares of common stock representing 27.5% of Tokyo Keiki's then issued and outstanding capital stock, made an uninvited attempt to acquire it. The attempt provoked such strong opposition, not only from Tokyo Keiki's management, but also from the Mitsubishi Bank, which was its main bank, and from the Mitsubishi Group of companies, that Tokyo Keiki, under the leadership of the Mitsubishi Bank and with the assistance of the Mitsubishi Heavy Industries Group, was able to launch a successful scheme to increase its loyal shareholders and their holdings. In this case, Minebea's attempt merely secured a seat on Tokyo Keiki's board of directors – Minebea eventually parted with its entire holdings in the company.

In 1983, Minebea also planned to purchase a sizable number of the common shares of the Janome Sewing Machines Company through tender offer. However, strong opposition from the Saitama Bank, which at that time was Janome's second largest shareholder, forced the abandonment of the plan before it even got off the ground.

Minebea's three unsuccessful attempts provide a good lesson for American or European potential investors: without discreet groundwork, attempts at American-style hostile acquisitions have virtually no chance of success in Japan.

2.4.2 The Misawa Homes Group: Friendly acquisition attempts

There are some corporations in Japan which have grown, or are growing, rapidly through mergers and acquisitions. A good example is that of the Misawa Homes Group, headed by Misawa Homes Co. Ltd, the nation's largest manufacturer and supplier of prefabricated housing units, materials, and components. Presently, the group is trying to develop toward being a supplier of integrated housing systems rather than being merely a manufacturer and supplier of prefabricated housing units. The company is one of the few in Japan which is very serious about acquisitions. Mr Chiyoji Misawa, its president, has stated that, in his opinion, the company must advance into such high-tech fields as "robotics, new industrial materials, biotechnology, and alternative sources of energy" to enable it to continue to grow as a profitable enterprise beyond the 21st century, and that one of the quickest ways to do this on a profitable basis is to "acquire shares in existing companies which already have proven technical and engineering bases in such fields." The group's expansion has been very rapid and quite remarkable: it has bought out a number of corporations, at a rate of two or more each year, all through friendly acquisitions. But why has this business philosophy never encountered any severe criticism?

Misawa Homes made its first acquisition in 1983, in the form of the Suzuki Iron Works Co. Ltd, which was then engaged in the manufacture of engineering machinery; Suzuki's common shares were listed on the Second Section of the Tokyo Stock Exchange. After the acquisition, Suzuki was successfully converted and restructured into a company specializing in computer hardware and software, and its corporate name was changed to Misawa VAN Co. Ltd. The company is now a supplier of real-estate data, including price information, primarily to the real-estate industry.

In 1984, Misawa successfully acquired Hamano Industries Co. Ltd, also a listed company on the Second Section of the Tokyo Stock Exchange. Hamano, which had been a manufacturer of chemicals for use by paper manufacturers, was then successfully converted and restructured into a developer and manufacturer of new or advanced building materials, including plastic-reinforced cement and highly heat-resistant fine ceramics.

In 1985, Misawa successfully acquired the Toyo Bosuifu Mfg. Co. Ltd, a manufacturer of vinyl leather and rubber products, also listed on the Second Section of the Tokyo Stock Exchange. Toyo Bosuifu is now engaged primarily in the development of new biotechnological products for household applications.

These three acquisition cases have some important features in common. First of all, the three target companies were either in financial distress or troubled by rigging attempts by groups of speculative investors, or both. As far as they were concerned, Misawa came to their rescue as a "white knight" in shining armor. Suzuki was virtually bankrupt, while Hamano, which had been unprofitable and unable to declare dividends for several years, was making desperate efforts to defeat another hostile acquisition attempt. The Toyo Bosuifu common shares were also the target of rigging attempts by groups of speculative investors, and the company was making desperate efforts to defeat these attempts.

Second, Misawa was very considerate and thoughtful with regard to the employees of the acquired companies. To take the acquisition of Suzuki as an example, Mr Misawa met the entire Suzuki workforce – over 100 employees – personally at the time of the negotiations: meetings lasted for two full days, and he was finally able to persuade them to agree to the proposed acquisition. The pattern was repeated when Misawa Homes acquired Hamano. "Though corporations are owned by their shareholders," he repeatedly remarked, "in Japan, traditionally management, as well as the general public, consider that the employees are more important than the shareholders. I understand that it is a generally accepted common practice for corporations in America or Europe to lay off their employees before the corporation becomes so unprofitable as to be unable to declare dividends. The reverse is generally true in Japan. If you want to be really successful in making mergers and acquisitions in Japan, the first thing you must do above all is to persuade and get the support of the employees of the target companies."

In October 1986, Misawa Homes invested in Nisseki Housing Industries Co. Ltd, and acquired 0.95% of its issued and outstanding common shares. Nisseki was a manufacturer of prefabricated housing units, specializing in steel-framed middle-rise apartments, while Misawa specialized in houses for single families. The Misawa management felt that both companies complemented each other, and decided to invest in and cooperate with Nisseki in the development of steel-framed prefabricated housing units for single families, and joint purchasing and marketing activities.

In 1987, Misawa became more acquisition-minded than ever. In January it acquired 19.6% of the issued and outstanding common shares of Suido Kiko Co. Ltd, a drainage and water supply contractor whose shares were traded on the over-the-counter market, and became Suido Kiko's largest shareholder. With Misawa's equity participation providing the momentum, Suido Kiko is now expected to progress into the development of new sewerage and water supply systems for residential homes, including integrated energy supply systems using underground water sources.

In February 1987, Misawa acquired 35.3% of the issued and outstanding common shares of Nippon Eternit Pipe, a manufacturer of concrete products whose common shares are listed on the First Section of the Tokyo Stock Exchange, and became its largest single shareholder. Misawa has announced that it will develop Nippon Eternit Pipe as its leisure industry division, primarily in the development and operation of golf clubs and other resort facilities. The company is now constructing a number of golf courses, mostly in the Kanto District, and also developing resort villages with hotels and other accommodation facilities.

In March 1987, Misawa purchased from Asahi Diamond Industries Co. Ltd 29% of the issued and outstanding common shares of Ishii Precision Tools Co. Ltd, a manufacturer of precision cutting tools whose common shares are listed on the Second Section of the Tokyo Stock Exchange. As a result of this purchase, it replaced Asahi Diamond Industries as Ishii's largest single shareholder and virtually obtained control of Ishii's management. Ishii's performance for the year ending March 1987 had been so poor, with such a huge operational loss, that it was not expected to issue an annual dividend. Further restructuring is now expected.

"Though our main business is building houses," Mr Misawa once remarked, "we should not limit our activities to that alone. We regard ourselves as developers and builders of new villages or towns. This concept requires us to extend our activities to the development of virtually everything that our communities need, including leisure facilities and services." To Misawa Homes, mergers and acquisitions are not only helpful in achieving active diversification, but so far have also proven to be very profitable indeed. For example, Toyo Bosuifu's premises in Itabashi, Tokyo, are said to have a market value of over ¥8 billion, against their book value of less than ¥50 million. If Toyo Bosuifu can successfully relocate its plant and redevelop the site for housing, it will be able to realize a significant capital gain from which Misawa can, of course, benefit considerably.

In addition, the market prices of the shares of the companies acquired by Misawa, particularly those whose common shares were listed on the Second Section of the Tokyo Stock Exchange, at least doubled within a relatively short period of time after their acquisition, while they had been at very depressed levels before acquisition. Not only can Misawa enjoy great benefits by becoming an assets-rich company, able to raise funds using its holdings in those companies as collateral, but the fact that their stock prices on the market remain at relatively high levels also makes it easier for the companies in the Misawa Group to raise funds from the capital market.

3

Mergers and Acquisitions: Japanese Style

As mentioned in Chapter 2, it is expected that the number of mergers and acquisitions in Japan will increase rapidly. There are two factors which endorse the view that an increasing number of Japanese companies will seek to sell their subsidiaries and/or introduce equity capital from outside sources during the years to come.

First, as the basic structure of Japan's economy continues to change, an increasing number of Japanese companies will be required to actively restructure their operations, with financial assistance from outside sources. Second, in line with the current international economic trend, an increasing number of major Japanese companies will be required to pursue the international division of labor more actively than ever to achieve future growth; and this will cause a number of subsidiaries or suppliers to become surplus to requirements.

It is interesting to speculate how mergers and acquisitions of Japanese companies by foreign corporations will develop. It is entirely possible that they will increase steadily, but not if foreign corporations continue to attempt American-style acquisitions.

The current Japanese legal system is not impenetrable; in fact, it is open to mergers and acquisitions by foreign investors.

Apparent obstacles or barriers have more to do with the Japanese reaction to hostile or high-handed transactions. It is not the purpose of this book to discuss the best way of doing business. The only thing that can be said with any certainty is that if foreign investors want to succeed they must get the Japanese on their side.

3.1 LESSONS FROM THE PAST

It is more practical, I believe, for foreign corporations seeking success to learn from past failures than to study the criteria for success. Readers must, however, bear in mind that the following discussion does not represent any systematic or theoretic analysis of all the typical past failures. These examples are merely intended to give readers some empirical lessons from my own personal experience, so that they will not make the same mistakes.

As the events discussed below occurred very recently, the parties involved will remain anonymous, and fact has sometimes been supplemented by just a little fiction!

3.1.1 The careless use of "acquisition"

An American manufacturer of special-purpose semiconductors desired to expand and promote the sale of its products in Japan, and was seriously considering acquiring one of its Japanese competitors. The target company had several problems of its own at the time. First, its performance had been unsatisfactory for several years. Second, its R & D had so far been unsuccessful. Third, its president and chairman of the board (the principal owner) had no son or daughter who could inherit the company. One of the acquiring company's local banks in Japan was asked to explore the possibility of acquiring a Japanese company. The bank, which happened to know of a suitable target company, established contact with the principal owner and arranged a confidential and informal meeting with him to explore the possibility.

Initially they exchanged views about possible ways of improving the target company's performance. Then they proceeded to discuss the possibility of the target company's establishing business and/or equity relations with a major corporation, whether Japanese or foreign, as an alternative way of achieving future growth. Finally, after a series of meetings, the principal owner confided to the bank that he felt that the future of his company was very gloomy, unless some drastic action was taken; and that because he had no son or daughter, he would be willing to sell his stake in the company to the acquiring company, if the latter were to make an attractive offer. He also added that since he was highly regarded within the industry, he would not be willing to sell his entire stake to any acquiring company in one outright sale. If there was a legitimate offer from a reputable company, he would initially be willing to establish cooperative business relations with the potential purchaser, including partial equity participation in his company. Ultimately, if such relations proved successful, he would be willing to negotiate the possible sale of his remaining stake in the company after three years or so. Furthermore, he had not told anyone in his company, including the senior managing director, that he was thinking of selling, for fear that if he did so, it would cause chaos amongst the company management, who would naturally not welcome any drastic changes. In order to avoid any confusion, he said he would prefer to tell the other managers that he was considering establishing a business tie-up between his company and the potential purchaser. Essentially, all he needed was enough time to persuade the other board members.

In October 1986, a formal meeting was arranged between the representatives of the two companies. Before the meeting, the acquiring company had been warned that the purpose of the meeting was to discuss the possibility of establishing business relations, and that they were not to discuss possible acquisition. A negotiation scenario was even prepared in line with this brief. At the meeting, the acquiring company was represented by its president, senior vice-president in charge of marketing, a certified public accountant from its outside auditors, and an American lawyer from its law firm, plus an interpreter, while the target company was represented by four people, including the principal owner. Unfortunately, the meeting lasted only ten minutes. Because of a lack of coordination on the part of the acquiring company, the American lawyer carelessly used the English word "acquisition" in his opening statement to explain the position of his client. Naturally the word was translated by the interpreter into the Japanese *baishu*. Upon hearing this, the principal owner turned pale, said that he had not come to "sell the company," and abruptly walked out of the meeting. There were no further talks, and the negotiations came to a complete end.

3.1.2 Failure due to an initial mismatch

This case involved a company based in Saitama Prefecture which was engaged primarily in the business of manufacturing special steel (the target company), and a major Japanese manufacturer and supplier of industrial materials (the acquiring company). The target company was one of the leading companies in the industry and was well known for its positive R & D efforts. However, its performance had been unsatisfactory for several years because orders from one of its major customers, one of the nation's largest automobile manufacturers, were falling substantially. The president of the company came to the conclusion that, in order to overcome its difficulties and secure future growth, it should not hesitate to take the opportunity of coming under the control of a reliable major company. He therefore contacted the marketing director of the acquiring company directly to explore the possibility. By coincidence, the marketing division of the acquiring company was seriously considering expanding its operations into the downstream end of the market, and had just started acquisition negotiations with one of the target company's competitors (the competing company). Having been offered this opportunity to obtain shares in the target company, the marketing division of the acquiring company conducted a careful comparative study, and reached the conclusion that the competing company was more attractive, primarily because it had a larger annual steel product sales revenue than the target company. Having come to this conclusion, the marketing division declined the target company's offer.

While its marketing division was busy studying this potential acquisition, the acquiring company's corporate headquarters, which was also seriously considering a similar expansion as part of its diversification plans, developed its own scheme and appointed an *ad hoc* new business development committee to select possible acquisition targets on a rather discreet basis. Due to poor intracompany communications, neither the marketing division nor this committee had a chance to find out about the other's activities.

A commercial bank was then consulted by the president of the target company and was asked to find a reliable company which was interested in a potential purchase. Before this could be done, the same bank was contacted by the headquarters of the acquiring company in connection with the proposed acquisition of the manufacturer.

Consequently, the bank introduced the target company to the acquiring company's *ad hoc* committee as a potential acquisition target. The committee, which showed great interest in acquiring the target company because of the latter's potential engineering ability to develop new special steel, reevaluated it from a fresh angle and tried to obtain an intracompany consensus. Eventually, however, this failed to materialize because the marketing division stuck firmly to its guns and insisted that the target company had already been evaluated and rejected.

This case exemplifies the lack of interdivisional coordination which is often evident in Japanese companies, and how difficult it is to reverse a business decision once it is made. It also suggests that to sell a company successfully it is vitally important to make the right decision as to how and to whom a selling offer is to be made. Similarly, the most important key to success in acquiring a company is to make the right decision as to how and to whom a purchase offer is to be made.

3.1.3 Inadequate respect for the problems of "losing face"

As is often said, the problem of "losing face" is very important to Japanese businessmen. In this case, the acquiring company, which was inexperienced in mergers and acquisitions, antagonized the target company and totally spoiled the negotiations because of its lack of respect for the Oriental virtue of modesty or "respecting one's elders," and the too outspoken concern it expressed about the economic terms of the proposed deal. The case involved a major American food manufacturing company which was actively expanding its operations in Japan into peripheral fields (the acquiring company) and a middle-sized manufacturer of processed food materials (the target company), which was also engaged in the import of food products: although it had an invaluable intangible asset in its high number of good customers, its annual sales revenues and profits had been poor for several years because of its lack of "hit" products. In addition, its owner and president was old enough to retire, and was thinking of selling the company to a reliable enterprise which was willing to assure him of the continued security of all the officers and employees.

One of the target company's banks was consulted by the president, and the bank then introduced him to the acquiring company. The first problem was where to hold the meeting between the two chief executive officers. The bank recommended that the president of the acquiring company, which was in a stronger bargaining position and had greater resources, should visit the president of the target company out of courtesy and respect. The acquiring company did not accept this advice, saying that their president's schedule was too tight. Thus the president of the target company visited the president of the acquiring company at the latter's office in the US. At their first meeting, the president of the acquiring company, who did not mention his considerable interest in the strong marketing team and good customers that the target company had built up, tried to spend as much time as possible discussing the economic terms and conditions of the proposed deal, in an obvious attempt to buy the target company as cheaply as possible. On the other hand, the president of the target company was ready to accept any reasonable offer as long as his greatest concern – the continued security of his employees – could be satisfied.

At a second meeting, the president of the acquiring company again spent much of his time criticizing the weaknesses, particularly the financial weakness, of the target company, without showing a hint of admiration for the strong marketing team. By now, the president of the target company felt that not only he but also the company to which he had dedicated his whole life had been unfairly insulted and openly disgraced and, to make matters worse, in the presence of the other members of the board of directors, most of whom he had personally trained from apprenticeship onward. Already disgusted because he had been forced to travel to the US for the first meeting instead of the other way round, he became furious and immediately called off the meeting – and so matters came to an abrupt end.

To have achieved success, the president of the acquiring company should have been more considerate. In fact, the acquiring company's attitude toward the negotiations at the first meeting had already convinced the bank that the officers and employees of the target company would not get along with the acquiring company's management, and that the negotiations would be discontinued sooner or later.

3.1.4 The perils of impatience

In this typical case the acquiring company lost the target company to a competitor because of its inflexible acquisition strategy, and its inability to take an alternative course of action. A major European machine tool company (the acquiring company) was eager to implement its operational program to improve and strengthen its robotics business worldwide. The main objective of the program, started three years previously, was to concentrate on the manufacture and supply of high-grade products with good profit margins. The company was very anxious to establish a local source of supply in Japan, through which it could increase its share of the Japanese market. Since Japanese customers have more stringent demands with regard to quality and performance than their counterparts elsewhere in the world, including America and Europe, the management considered that if they could satisfy their Japanese customers, and prove their ability beyond doubt, their reputation could be enhanced considerably outside Japan. Another reason for establishing a local source of supply in Japan was to give Japanese customers direct access to the production lines and facilities, thus convincing them of the quality of the product. The company therefore instructed its nonmanufacturing Japanese subsidiary to identify a potential acquisition target from among the reputable Japanese manufacturers. By "acquisition" the head office meant the purchase of more than a 50% interest. The Japanese subsidiary repeatedly told its head office that this would be no easy task, that it would take quite some time to obtain a controlling interest, and that the best plan of action would be to acquire a minority interest in the first instance. However, head-office staff, who had encountered no significant difficulties in acquiring robot manufacturers in other parts of the world, including the US and NICs countries, paid little heed to their subsidiary's warnings, and actually criticized it for reacting too slowly.

At that time, the target company, a medium-sized Japanese industrial robot manufacturer, with factories in Osaka, was facing such keen price competition that its profitability was seriously eroded and its future was becoming increasingly gloomy, with diminishing funds available to finance R & D activities. Its management was divided into two camps, one in favor of the idea of curtailing operations for a while to make the company profitable again, and the other in favor of the company's being taken under a major corporate umbrella. Although the company president, who had only recovered from illness a couple of months earlier, was in favor of the latter strategy – either through equity or nonequity relations – primarily to secure the jobs of his employees, and to generate much-needed R & D resources, particularly in view of the rapid technical innovations in the industry, he was aware that no consensus had yet been reached among the board members.

At the request of the acquiring company, one of its banks contacted the target company and was told by the president that although he was very interested in accepting the offer to purchase the controlling interest in his company, particularly in view of the success of a new medical product introduced recently by the acquiring company and because of its superior R & D resources, he was not ready to accept the offer in view of possible fierce opposition from his board of directors. Also, from his company's point of view, it would be better to start with a licensor/licensee relationship under the acquiring company's patents or proprietary know-how, and/or a subcontractor relationship, with his company acting as the acquiring company's local manufacturing agent, with no equity participation. He felt that a relationship along these lines should be maintained for a year or two, during which time he would try to persuade the other board members to accept the acquiring company as one of its major shareholders. Accordingly, the bank recommended to the acquiring company's local subsidiary that it should start business on this basis, and that it should not demand shares until the target company's sales to the acquiring company and its affiliates, or sales of the products licensed by the acquiring company, formed a substantial proportion of its total sales. This would give the president of the target company enough time and sufficient evidence to convince the other board members. The subsidiary, which had always been convinced that the target company was the best potential acquisition, recommended to its head office that the target company should be granted a license to manufacture under the acquiring company's patents, as its local manufacturing subcontractor. Head office replied that while they agreed broadly with their subsidiary's view, operational pressures in other parts of the world meant that they could not delay equity participation for more than six months. With no option but to try to implement this instruction, the subsidiary came back to the president of the target company and unsuccessfully offered a package deal consisting of equity participation, the granting of a patent license, and the appointment of the target company as local manufacturing subcontractor.

Three months later, the target company publicly announced that it had entered into a business tie-up with a major Japanese company, and that under that arrangement it was going to accept several senior executives from the other company onto its board.

3.2 USEFUL NEGOTIATING TECHNIQUES

In mergers and acquisitions in Japan, as in any other part of the world, one of the most crucial issues during final negotiations is the fixing of the purchase price of the shares. It is also important to determine how the target company's employees will be treated. There is also a further, very difficult joint task to be accomplished: how to persuade the principal shareholders of the target company to sell their shares to the acquiring company. In Japan, distinctly different negotiating techniques are needed, and the difference lies in a significant emphasis on emotional persuasion.

The most difficult task for an acquiring company, or the M & A consultant or broker acting on its behalf, is to persuade these principal shareholders to commit themselves to selling their shares – considerable prudence and great care must be exercised. Furthermore, the techniques used must depend on the nature of the target company. Roughly speaking, target companies fall into one of the following three categories:

1 *Type A*   a company with serious financial problems, and badly in need of rescue, which has expressed its willingness to be acquired.
2 *Type B*   a company in good financial condition which is strongly opposed to any acquisition attempts. The offer of a business tie-up is the best approach in this case, in the hope that the relationship will eventually lead to reduced hostility to potential acquisition.
3 *Type C*   a company which may be willing to be acquired, but which has not publicly expressed any such willingness. It is almost impossible to force a company of this type into a state of willingness.

When acquiring a Type A company, the economic terms of the deal and the speed with which arrangements can be completed are of paramount importance. No other special considerations are usually necessary. In that sense, the acquiring company can and should proceed in the American fashion. If the continued service and assistance of the target company's management after acquisition are envisaged, some provision must be made to respect the dignity of its current president; and the security of all, or most, of the current employees must also be guaranteed.

It is virtually impossible to acquire a Type B company in Japan. It is not worth trying. Even if the target company was listed, a tender offer would not meet with success because of the influence of "stable major shareholders," usually banks or other financial institutions. Such shareholders are invariably on friendly terms with the management of the listed companies in which they have invested. With few exceptions, it is impossible to acquire more than 50% of the stock of any listed company against the stable major shareholders' will. It is even difficult, although not impossible, to acquire minority ownership in a company of this type. Because of the criticism to which he would be subjected, no broker or funding agent would be prepared to cooperate. Therefore, a potential investor hoping to acquire a Type B company must be patient and have a long-term perspective. It should begin with a distributorship, licensing, or long-term supply arrangement to gain the confidence of its potential target; and to place itself in a prime position to come to the financial assistance of the target company if necessary.

Japanese-style negotiating techniques are particularly in demand when attempting to acquire a Type C company. Such an acquisition would indeed be challenging, particularly if the target company is very attractive in terms of its marketing and merchandising abilities, its goodwill, and its technical and engineering capabilities. The key to success depends on technique. Carelessness would simply antagonize the target company and provoke a flat refusal. The best approach would be to offer to help the company expand or strengthen its operational bases, or improve its R & D capabilities, marketing forces, or financial resources. And the words "acquisition," "takeover," and "merger" are taboo!

In most cases, even a successful approach would not result in immediate equity participation or acquisition. But as long as some continuing business relation is established and maintained, there is always a good chance of expansion toward an equity or, ultimately, a parent–subsidiary relationship. When an initial approach is made toward a Type C company, careful precautions must be taken to conceal the long-term intention to acquire. But as negotiations or business relations develop, it becomes necessary at some stage to suggest the real intention to the target company, and at the same time it is vital that the acquiring company finds out whether or not the target is willing to be acquired. This requires considerable delicacy, and provides a real challenge for M & A consultants or brokers. In Japan, important business decisions are often still made outside the office after office hours, perhaps over a few drinks or at a dinner party. Therefore consultants or brokers have to make very intelligent use of their time. It is vital to hedge around direct questions, because a direct approach will often put the opponent on the defensive. As the old proverb says, "Tell without being asked." If you want to know what someone else is really thinking, try to be as open-minded as possible – and be prepared to swallow your pride first – so that your opponent will open his heart and disclose his real thoughts. This is what the proverb really means. It is one of the keys to success in Japan, because emotion, rather than logic, is the main guiding force. Once the owner or principal shareholder admits that he truly intends to sell his stake in the company, negotiations often proceed very smoothly; and logic comes into its own – although some emotional problems may remain. Once the commitment has been obtained, over drinks or the dinner table, call it a day. Sleep on that commitment, meet again the next morning to obtain confirmation, and then go on to discuss the detailed terms and conditions of the deal.

When negotiating mergers or acquisitions in Japan, it is always advisable to use the services of a good M & A consultant or broker. When the acquiring and target companies meet directly, it is often difficult to make substantive progress. Even if discussions do become open-minded, there is always the risk that some seemingly minor incident will lead to serious disruption, and the consultant's or broker's role as mediator is then vital. His most important task is to persuade both parties to reveal their true intentions. While he must have excellent professional knowledge of the industries or technologies in question, there is little doubt that his interpersonal skills are of paramount importance.

3.3 CONTACT THE RIGHT PEOPLE

The keys to success in Japanese mergers and acquisitions is often the correct resolution of the delicate matter of who should make the initial approach to whom. An inadvisable initial contact can ruin the entire process of negotiation.

The correct formalities have to be observed, and acquisition negotiations have to be conducted at the highest level (this is, of course, true not only in Japan but throughout the business world). If your contact does not have the real authority to see negotiations through, your attempt may easily be frustrated by the target company, particularly by middle-ranking target company executives who feel that they have been passed over, and consequently are keen to become involved in corporate decision-making. Therefore, before you make your initial approach, you must research the target company very carefully. Consider the following example.

An American manufacturer of chemical products had, for some years, enjoyed a close business relationship with a similar Japanese manufacturer. The engineers in both companies had frequent opportunities to liaise, and they eventually concluded that an even closer relationship would be to their mutual benefit. However, one of the Japanese engineers knew that his immediate superior, the chief engineer, was the leader of a faction within the company that opposed outside intervention, and preferred to develop the company's R & D capabilities independently. Furthermore, the engineer was not brave enough to go over his superior's head and approach opposing factions, or the company president, directly. Therefore, he consulted a commercial bank for advice. The bank conducted a thorough investigation of the various factions within the company, in order to select its initial contact properly: it chose to approach the senior executive director, who was the leader of a neutral faction, and who had considerable influence over the president. In addition, the bank prepared various scenarios to convince the company's management that it would benefit from the proposed tie-up, and was able to present their case as if the whole undertaking had been entered into at the request of the American company. This tactic was successful, and consequently resulted in a mutually beneficial arrangement.

While it seems to make most sense to approach the chief executive officer in the first instance, it is often more important to find out who has the real power and authority, or is considered to be most reliable, and which of the top managers of the target company should be recruited as your allies. A thorough investigation is essential: in a Japanese company bottom-up decision-making (represented by the *ringuisho*, a kind of presentation paper) is commonplace, rather than the top-down process which is more familiar in the US or Europe.

4

Selection and Evaluation of a Target Japanese Company

As mentioned earlier, in Japan acquisition of a company is generally considered to be a means of achieving reorganization or restructuring. In American and European practice, one of the most important criteria for selecting and evaluating acquisition targets is the short-term profitability, or price earning ratio (PER). However, this is not always the case in Japan: Japanese companies cannot always be properly evaluated on this basis – and good potential targets would often be overlooked. In Japan, additional selection criteria must be used. But why should this be?

4.1 PRICE EARNING RATIO (PER)

In American and European practice, PER is often used as an evaluation criterion. PER is determined by dividing the current market price of the company's common stock by its common share earnings after tax. The earnings per share after tax and PER are inversely related to each other: the lower the one, the higher the other. The average PERs of all stocks listed on the First Section of the Tokyo Stock Exchange and on the New York Stock Exchange over a certain period are shown in Table 4.1.

Selection and Evaluation of a Target Company

Table 4.1 Annual variation of PER, US and Japan

Year	Japan	US
1975	27.0	12.4
1976	46.3	11.5
1977	24.2	9.1
1978	34.3	8.7
1979	23.3	7.9
1980	20.4	7.9
1981	21.1	8.7
1982	25.8	8.2
1983	34.7	11.2
1984	37.9	9.0
1985	35.2	10.5
1986	47.3	13.5
1987	54.7	14.7

Note: Japan, Tokyo Stock Exchange; US, New York Stock Exchange.
Source: The Tokyo Stock Exchange *Monthly Statistical Report,* published by the
Tokyo Stock Exchange

Table 4.2 Stock price comparison of major countries

Country	PER	PBR	Dividend yield (%)
Japan	55.9	4.64	0.5
US	17.4	2.10	3.1
UK	15.0	2.19	3.6
FDR	13.0	2.26	3.3
France	20.1	2.35	2.3
Canada	22.5	1.92	2.4
Italy	20.0	2.37	1.8
World	21.9	2.51	2.2

Source: Morgan Stanley Capital International Perspective

4.2 PRICE BOOK RATIO (PBR)

Another ratio often used during evaluation is the price book ratio (PBR). This is determined by dividing the current market price of the company's common stock by the book value (the shareholders' equity) per common share. The average PBR of all stocks listed on the First Section of the Tokyo Stock Exchange in 1987 was 3.5, almost twice as high as the values on other major world stock exchanges in the same year. The average values of PER and PBR on the seven major world stock markets at the end of March 1987 are shown in Table 4.2.

Why are the PERs and PBRs of Japanese companies so high? The answer lies in hidden or undervalued assets.

4.3 HIDDEN OR UNDERVALUED ASSETS

As explained above, PBR is the ratio between the actual stock price and its book value (net assets value). In most cases, the value of land owned by Japanese companies, as shown on the balance sheet, does not represent a fair market value: property is usually undervalued. The difference, the "hidden" or "undervalued" assets, is often so great that overseas investors find it difficult to digest. To clarify the situation, let us assume that a company with a business history going back over 50 years owns several attractive parcels of land in central Tokyo, or in other major cities and industrial zones, and that this land was all acquired before or shortly after World War II. The land is shown at cost on the balance sheet; however, there has been a tremendous increase in the price of land in Japan over recent decades, with the result that the book value is far below the current market value. In other words, the company has a huge amount of unrealized or "paper" profit, which is not reflected in its balance sheet.

65

As an example, consider the Okamura Corporation. According to its balance sheet at the end of November 1986, Okamura's total assets amounted to ¥69.4 billion, while the market value of its common stock was ¥665; hence the total market value of its issued and outstanding shares was a little under ¥50 billion. Amongst other properties, Okamura owned a 9,400 square meter parcel of land in Yokohama. The market value of this single tract of land at the time was in excess of ¥90 billion – far greater than the aggregate market value of the company's issued and outstanding common shares.

Another good example is the Iino Shipping Co. Ltd. Iino's trading performance in recent years has been very poor, reflecting the worldwide recession in the shipping industry. On the Tokyo Stock Exchange, the closing price of the company's common stock on September 30, 1986 was ¥770, making the aggregate market value of its entire issued and outstanding stock approximately ¥73.9 billion on that day. However, Iino owned an attractive tract of land, of 7,600 or so square meters, in the Hibiya area, one of the best business centers in Tokyo, with a current market value of at least ¥30 million per square meter, or approximately ¥230 billion in total!

An extreme example is provided by the Seibu Railway Group, owned by Mr Yoshiaki Tsutumi and his family, and particularly its quasi-holding company, Kokudo Keikaku Co. Ltd. Mr Tsutumi is said to be the richest person in the world today: Kokudo Keikaku owns almost two-thirds of the land used by the Seibu Railway Group, approximately 37,000 acres, with a fair market value of more than ¥12 trillion. This can be compared to the total assets value of ¥116.2 billion, as shown in the company's most recent balance sheet. Most of the land was acquired over 40 years ago, and its book value is negligible compared to the current market value.

The Mitsubishi Real Estate Co. Ltd owns substantially all of the Marunouchi area, Japan's most prestigious business center. According to a recent survey, the aggregate current market value of all land owned by Mitsubishi Real Estate, including its Marunouchi investments, amounted to ¥4 trillion – and recent land price inflation has increased that figure by at least a quarter. Mitsubishi Real Estate's share price hit the ceiling in August 1986, when it peaked at ¥2,550. Hence the aggregate market value of its issued and outstanding shares, ¥3 trillion, compared to the aggregate market value of its land, left a residue of "hidden assets" amounting to ¥1 trillion.

Land is not the only form of "hidden asset." These days, almost all companies invest on the stock market as part of their "assets management." In addition, a number of companies have maintained reciprocal or mutual equity relations for a number of years. According to generally accepted accounting principles, shares are stated on the balance sheet at either cost or market value, whichever is the lower. Generally speaking, shares are stated at a substantially lower level than their current market price, even after "Black Monday" in 1987. Thus shares in other companies represent a very considerable portion of "hidden assets."

4.4 SALES OUTLETS: INVALUABLE GOODWILL

Distribution systems in Japan are very complicated, and so any firm with successful sales outlets in Japan should be viewed as having invaluable goodwill; which is often substantially undervalued by American and European investors, who are used to relatively simple systems. The high degree of complexity, redundancy, and interdependence which characterizes Japanese distribution systems makes it relatively easy for established companies to maintain the volume of their business, while it is extremely difficult for newcomers to break into the market. Therefore it is very important to ensure that potential American or European investors properly evaluate their Japanese target firm's sales outlets and marketing organization.

Table 4.3 Numbers of outlets (or firms) and employees, and sales revenues, of wholesalers in major countries

	No. of outlets or firms[a]	Employees (persons)	Sales revenues
Japan 1972	O 259,163	3,007,647	¥106,780,082 million
1982	O 428,858	4,090,919	¥395,536,234 million
US 1972	O 369,791	4,026,118	US$695,224 million
1982	O 415,829	4,984,880	US$1,997,895 million
UK 1974	F 80,100	1,023,000	£51,170 million
1983	F 104,688	1,125,000	£141,461 million
France 1972	F 60,012	667,874	Fr229,716 million[b]
1982	F 77,605	925,595	Fr1,225,797 million[b]
1975	O 112,932		
1984	O 134,320		
FDR 1968	F 111,986	1,210,247	DM246,515 million
1979	F 97,707	1,160,860	DM613,352 million
1968	O 123,245		
1979	O 119,567		

Notes:
[a] F – firms; O – outlets.
[b] After deduction of value-added taxes.
Source: International Comparative Study of Distribution Systems (Ryutsu no Kokusai Hikaku Kenkyu Hokokusyo), Distribution Policies Research Institute

As elsewhere in the world, merchandise travels from the manufacturer to the wholesaler, and then to the retailer. What makes the Japanese market unique is that the wholesale sector often consists of two or more tiers. Comparisons of the number of wholesale establishments in various countries, the number of employees in the wholesale sector, and the sector's annual turnover are shown in Table 4.3: for the dates indicated, Japan and the US had approximately 400,000 wholesale establishments each, whereas the UK, France, and West Germany had about 100,000 each. Given the size of Japan's economy

Table 4.4 Ratio of number of wholesale outlets and number of retail outlets for consumer goods in major countries

	Japan (1982)	US (1982)	France (1982)[a]	FDR (1979)
Wholesale outlets (A)	213,253	154,004	53,274	66,587
Retail outlets (B)	1,721,465	1,807,000	398,168	412,714
B / A	8.1	11.7	7.5	6.2

Note:
[a] Data based on the number of companies.
Sources:
Japan, *Trade Statistics Table 1982*
US, *Census of Wholesale Trade 1982* and *Census of Retail Trade 1982*
France, *Enquête annuelle d'enterprises dans le commerce 1982*
FDR, *Handels- und Gestattenzahlung 1979*

compared to that of the US, Japan had twice as many wholesale establishments as the US.

The numbers of retail establishments are compared in Table 4.4: Japan has substantially more than the US, France, and West Germany, which proves that Japan's retail sector is just as complex as the wholesale sector. One remarkable fact that Table 4.4 reveals is that, although Japan is only about one twenty-fifth the size of the US (in terms of geographical area), has only about half the population, and has a national economy that is only half as large, the number of retail establishments is about the same.

To supply these retail outlets, Japan had approximately 210,000 wholesale establishments that supplied consumer products, while the comparable number in the US was only 150,000 or so. Japanese wholesalers have intricate business relationships, not only among themselves but also with manufacturers and retailers. These exclusive distributorships, marketing agency relationships and long-established personal and equity relations often form business groups of an exclusive nature.

A small manufacturer with no nationwide marketing team has little option but to use the services of a major wholesaler or distributor who has a nationwide marketing network. This wholesaler or distributor then, in turn, uses the services of regional or local distributors within, or associated with, his group to sell the products to local "subdistributors" or retailers.

One of the characteristics that distinguish Japanese distribution systems from their American and European counterparts is that while the latter tend to care more about consumers than manufacturers ("The customer is always right"), the former tend to be concerned more about the manufacturers that they represent than the consumers whom they should serve. It follows that while US and European distributors tend to select merchandise on the basis of feedback from consumers or other end users, their counterparts in Japan tend to be influenced more by manufacturers' marketing policy. Inevitably, while in America or Europe retailers exercise considerable influence over wholesalers and manufacturers, in Japan the wholesalers and retailers tend to form exclusive business groups, centered around the manufacturers whom they represent – and backed up in most cases by equity relations. Looking from the retail end of the chain, it is not difficult to conclude that the entire Japanese system is controlled by the manufacturers: even to the extent that indigenous Japanese manufacturers, including companies of long standing, often find it difficult to sell products when they attempt to enter a new market through diversification or otherwise.

However, within this complex system there exist very good opportunities for American or European firms that wish to enter the Japanese market. The successful acquisition of a Japanese manufacturer or wholesaler almost certainly brings with it that controlling power over downstream operations, and that same invaluable goodwill, whether or not it is properly reflected in the balance sheet.

Merck's acquisition of Banyu Pharmaceutical (reputed to have cost US$314 million), which took place in August 1983, provides a case in point. Merck had started doing business in Japan as early as December 1954 when, with Banyu, it organized a joint venture company, Nippon Merck Banyu Co. Ltd. The primary objective of the 1983 acquisition was to secure Banyu's nationwide distribution system: it is well known that the pharmaceutical industry in Japan has a complex network. Following the acquisition, Merck merged Nippon Merck Banyu into Banyu itself, and this surviving corporation now has a marketing force consisting of over 900 retail staff, the third largest in the Japanese pharmaceutical industry, next only to those of Shionogi and Takeda. This formidable organization now enables Merck to introduce and successfully market, within Japan, new products that were developed and approved in the US and Europe (see also Section 2.3).

4.5 GOVERNMENT LICENSES: INVALUABLE INTANGIBLE ASSETS

In many cases, Japanese companies operate under business licenses, permits, approvals, or concessions, invaluable intangible assets that seldom appear on the balance sheet. Unlike in the US, where private industry has been thoroughly deregulated by the Reagan Administration, or in Europe, where modern *laissez faire* capitalism was born, private businesses in Japan are often still subject to governmental license, because capitalism was first introduced in Japan during the Meiji era as one of a number of measures to reform and modernize the Japanese economy. While vigorous administrative reforms were undertaken by the Nakasone Administration, the government's authority to license was neither relaxed nor augmented in any way.

According to the 1988 Economic White Paper, Japanese industries are to remain subject to various forms of governmental

Table 4.5 Degree of governmental regulation, by industrial sector[a]

Industrial sector	Contribution of sector to total national industry (%)	Degree of regulation (%)	Principal regulations
Civil construction	6.8	100.0	Construction Business Act and Electric Work Industry Operations Improvement Act
Finance	5.2	100.0	Banking Act, Long-Term Credit Bank Act, Mutual Financing Bank Act, Securities and Exchange Act, Insurance Business Act, and Temporary Interest Adjustment Act
Power, gas, water supply	3.0	100.0	Electricity Supply Business Act, Gas Supply Business Act, Water Supply Business Act, and Sewage Business Act
Mining	0.4	100.0	Mining Act and Special Measurements for Coal Mining Act
Transport, telecommunications	6.1	96.3	Trucking Business Act, Railway Business Act, Aviation Act, and Telecommunication Business Act
Forestry, fishery	3.0	78.0	Staple Food Control Act, Vegetable Supply Stabilization Act, and Fishing Act
Service	10.7	29.8	Environmental Hygiene-Related Business Improvement Act, Hotel Business Act, Security Service Business Act, and Lawyers Act
Manufacture[b]	29.4	13.2	
Domestic market orientated	15.5	21.1	Liquor Tax Act, Livestock Products Price Stabilization Act, Petroleum Business Act, and Pharmaceutical Business Act
Overseas market orientated	13.8	4.3	Shipbuilding Act, Temporary Shipbuilding Operations Adjustment Act, Weapons Manufacturing Act, and Measuring and Weighing Act

Table 4.5 (cont.) Degree of governmental regulation, by industrial sector[a]

Industrial sector	Contribution of sector to total national industry (%)	Degree of regu- lation (%)	Principal regulations
Real estate	10.0	3.2	Residential Land and Building Trading Act
Public service, not classified	4.0	0	
Wholesale, retail	12.5	—[c]	
Total industry	100.0	33.6	

Notes:
[a] Figures derived on the basis of the *Inter-Industry Relations Table*. The calculation of the degree of governmental regulation, by industrial sector, as of July 1, 1988, is based upon the amount of value-addition for 1985.
[b] The overseas market oriented manufacturing industries include iron and steel, and machinery (including electric machinery, transport machinery, and precision machinery); the domestic market oriented manufacturing industries are those excluded in the overseas category.
[c] Degree of governmental regulation not specified.
Source: Economic White Paper, 1988

regulation or restriction. For example, in the financial industries such as banking, securities, and insurance, companies still face various stringent regulations such as restrictions placed on new entrants, expansion of business lines, modification of business interest rates, and the opening of new offices.

Other examples exist throughout all sectors of Japanese industrial activity. In the retail trade, large businesses such as supermarket chains are prohibited from freely opening new stores, fixing their own opening hours, or expanding floor space. In the construction industry, governmental regulations make it extremely difficult for any company or individual to newly enter the industry. In transportation, civil aviation, bus, taxi, trucking, and railway companies are all subject to similar regulations, and to additional restrictions on fare or tariff rates, service routes, and geographical service areas. In telecommunications and broadcasting, government regulations make it very difficult for new entrants to gain a foothold in the industry, and tariff rates are subject to governmental approval. Finally, in the pharmaceutical industry, the manufacture, testing, and marketing of pharmaceutical and medical products and equipment, as well as the handling and storage of unstable and toxic agents, must adhere to strict regulations.

Within each industrial sector listed above, the percentage of business activity that is still subject to or restricted by governmental regulations is shown in Table 4.5.

Potential foreign investors should note that, generally, this body of regulations or restrictions does not prohibit any person or corporation, whether domestic or foreign, from newly entering an industry or market through the acquisition of a company that is already trading, provided that it currently possesses a license or permit, or the necessary governmental approval.

4.6 IDEAL ACQUISITION TARGETS: PROBLEMS OF SUCCESSION

As mentioned earlier, the acquisition of firms that are in financial distress has traditionally been the most popular form of foreign investment, although it often involves considerable risk. To lessen this risk, potential investors should look for reasonably profitable acquisition targets, and Japanese firms that are having difficulty finding suitable successors to take over their management are ideal.

The time has now come for the first generation of modern Japanese businessmen, those who have become owners and chief executive officers since early postwar times, to retire and – in the traditional manner – hand down management of their corporations to the next generation. But this is not always possible. According to a survey of 40,000 firms, conducted during May through July 1985 by the Nippon Mutual Life Assurance Company (Nissei), to which 5,492 owners of major smaller-sized firms responded, 1,993 owners (36.3%) replied that, so far, they had been unable to find the right successor to take over the reins. Of those 1,993 firms, 35.1% were highly profitable, 40.7% were marginally profitable, and 39.2% were in a break-even situation.

One of the major causes of difficulty seemed to be that most owners wanted their sons or daughters to take over. In fact, 3,097 (56.4%) replied to that effect, while 270 (5%) wanted their grandchildren to succeed them, and 220 (4%) wanted responsibility to pass to brothers. In other words, 65.4% would choose direct lineal descendants, or relatives of the second degree or closer, as their successors.

While 30.9% of the respondents considered that normal retirement age would be the right time to go, it is interesting to note that 25.2% stated that it was their intention to retire as soon as it became difficult to cope properly with rapid changes in the business, economic, or social environment. On the basis of these statistics, a considerable number of major smaller-sized Japanese firms must now be affected by these difficulties, and many owners would rather sell to an outside investor than instal existing senior employees as management leaders (an example, already mentioned in Section 2.3, is that of Tokyo Kaken Co. Ltd, which was acquired by the American Rawpack Corporation).

4.7 ACQUISITION OF CORPORATIONS IN FINANCIAL DISTRESS

As explained in Sections 2.1 and 2.4.2 (in connection with the Misawa Homes Group), acquisitions of profitable corporations within Japan have been extremely rare. Few owners or managers of profitable corporations would be willing to sell, and hostile acquisitions of profitable firms are yet to gain favorable social recognition as legitimate business transactions. Indeed, the term "acquisition" has generally become synonymous in Japan with "acquisition of an unprofitable corporation," a course of action that would be welcomed by all parties – management, owners, stockholders, banks, suppliers, customers, creditors, and employees. Social commendation is a very important factor in Japan; and so social commendation of the acquiring company is usually considered to be the essential ingredient in eliminating or offsetting the "evil" aspects inherent in such transactions. As mentioned in Section 2.4.2, the Suzuki Iron Works, Hamano Industries, and Toyo Bosuifu Mfg. were all unprofitable at the time of acquisition by Misawa Homes.

Another Japanese corporation, Toyo Sash Co. Ltd, is well known for being equally acquisition-minded. Toyo Sash is a manufacturer of building materials, primarily window sashes. Although it had a substantial share of the market for window sashes for houses and low-rise apartments, it had no technical, engineering, or marketing base at all for curtain walls for high-rise buildings; and the company's own analysis indicated that it would take five to ten years at least for it to acquire a significant position in the curtain wall market, if it had to develop the required technology and marketing outlets on its own. At the same time, what was then the nation's largest curtain wall manufacturer, Nittetsu Curtain Walls Co. Ltd, had accumulated a staggering deficit of nearly ¥30 billion, despite its dominant position, with as much as 70% of the market. Toyo Sash successfully acquired Nittetsu Curtain Walls in 1986, and was able to acquire a substantial share of the high-rise building curtain wall market.

Toyo Sash did its research carefully, reaching the conclusion that Nittetsu could be made profitable again if its operating expenses were drastically curtailed, and if the products of

Nittetsu's house window sash division – its most unprofitable operation – were sold through Toyo's own sales outlets. This could be classified as a "reorganization promoting" acquisition. To induce Toyo Sash to acquire Nittetsu, the Japan Steel Corporation and Mitsui & Co. Ltd (Nittetsu's principal shareholders at the time) agreed to write off their loans and capital contributions to Nittetsu.

These examples indicate that it is important to consider the following: (i) whether or not there is confidence that an ailing company can be made profitable again within two to three years; (ii) whether or not positive assistance can be obtained from banks and existing principal shareholders (in the form of writing off of capital contributions and/or overdue loans, for example); and (iii) whether or not the acquisition is expected to bring about significant benefits that can offset the risks.

As mentioned in Section 2.1(2), in 1986 the Tokyo-based Heiwa Sogo Bank, which was one of the nation's largest mutual finance banks, merged with the Sumitomo Bank following serious financial difficulties, caused primarily by a huge inventory of bad debts which had accumulated over many years. An official MOF audit revealed that this included as much as ¥189 billion of nonperforming loans that would be difficult, if not impossible, to collect. Fearing a possible crisis, a substantial number of clients withdrew their deposits with the bank, making it even less creditworthy than it already was. Furthermore, internal strife among the board members was compounded by an ongoing criminal investigation by the public prosecutor's office into suspected illegal loan transactions. Even in such a critical situation, the MOF has a reputation for being determined to avoid the spectre of bankruptcy, and set out to search for a bank that could purchase and therefore rescue Heiwa Sogo.

The Sumitomo Bank, one of the nation's largest and most profitable banks, was well established in the Kansai area, including Osaka, but relatively weak in Tokyo. Despite Sumitomo's strong desire to expand, MOF restrictions had prevented the bank from opening new offices in the Tokyo area. On the other hand, at the time of the merger, Heiwa Sogo had 101 offices in Tokyo and its suburban areas. While this was obviously very attractive, Sumitomo was, of course, aware of Heiwa Sogo's bad debts, which it would have to assume in the event of a merger. However, there was a positive tradeoff, in the form of over ¥1,000 billion of outstanding deposits held on behalf of Heiwa Sogo's customers which, after transfer, would make Sumitomo second only to the Dai-Ichi Kangyo Bank in terms of the amount of deposits held. In addition, Sumitomo would acquire Heiwa Sogo's goodwill, and its reputation among the general public as the "most easily accessible" bank: this was important to Sumitomo's management, because it wished to dispel the general public's long-held view that it was somewhat high-handed in its operations, always pursuing a higher than average rate of return on assets.

It is interesting to note that Citibank had previously made an unsuccessful attempt to rescue Heiwa Sogo. The fact that the Sumitomo Bank was eventually chosen undoubtedly reflects the MOF's unannounced but obviously firm resolution that it will never allow a Japanese bank to be taken over by a foreign bank.

This is a good point at which to return to the history of Minebea's mergers and acquisitions in Japan. In 1974, Minebea successfully acquired the Shinko Tsushin Kogyo Company, a metal processing mills operator. In 1975, it acquired the Tokyo Screws Company, a manufacturer of screws and industrial fasteners, and the Shin Chuo Kogyo Company, a manufacturer of rotary machines and magnetic clutches. Finally, in 1976, it acquired the Osaka Wheels Mfg. Company, a manufacturer of automotive parts. At the time of acquisition, all four of these companies were unprofitable and unable to declare dividends. Minebea is believed to have acquired them primarily for the purpose of diversifying its own operations and, on a return to

78

profitability, in order to realize or take advantage of the value of the property that the four companies owned. Several years later, in 1979, Minebea acquired the Teikoku Die Casting Company, which was also in financial distress at the time.

As mentioned in Section 2.1(4), the giant Toshiba Corporation acquired the Sord Corporation in 1985. Sord had pioneered the manufacturing and marketing of personal computers in Japan, long before the big corporations – such as NEC, Toshiba, Matsushitsa, and IBM Japan – had entered the market. In the absence of competition, Sord grew very rapidly, and at its peak in 1983 what had been just a small business venture had developed into a medium-sized corporation with a paid-up share capital of ¥3.4 billion. Its original software product, "PIPS," was one of the best-selling software products in Japan at the time. In the face of subsequent keen competition, Sord lost its market share equally rapidly, and it was almost bankrupt by May 1985 when, for some ¥4 billion, Toshiba agreed to purchase (in the form of private placement) additional Sord common shares representing, upon completion, 50.1% of the company's issued and outstanding shares. In exchange Toshiba, which was a relatively late entrant in the personal computer market, indirectly acquired 5% of the market, and Sord's production, engineering, and design capabilities and facilities, including its powerful software development team of over 400 software engineers. A major disadvantage was that Toshiba had to assume Sord's losses of some ¥4.8 billion for the year ended February 1985. "Whether the acquisition of Sord is a good purchase for Toshiba or not," said Mr Morita, Sord's Toshiba-appointed executive vice-president, who was actively supervising Sord's day-to-day operations, "depends on how well we can manage and operate Sord from now on. I do not think it would be wise for Toshiba to exercise too much influence over Sord because it would hurt its independence as a venture business. From Toshiba's point of view, however, Sord should not be given so much independence or freedom as to allow it to fly out of orbit around Toshiba. Anyway, I'll do my best to make the acquisition a good purchase for Toshiba."

There is another large group of companies, the Seibu Saison Group (one of the two subgroups of the Seibu Group), which is well known for its positive acquisitions of companies with accumulated operating losses. In February 1984, Osawa & Co. Ltd, a medium-sized trading company known for its local distribution and export agencies for American-made "Ben Hogan" golf clubs, the German "Pogenpohl" and "Interlubke" system kitchen units, imported jewelry, and Japanese-made "Mamiya" cameras, became virtually bankrupt, with outstanding debts of ¥110 billion. Osawa subsequently filed a petition for reorganization, and its reorganization plan, which was supported by Seibu Saison's commitment to give financial, managerial, and operational assistance, was approved by the Tokyo District Court in September 1986. Immediately following this approval, Mr Eto, who at the time was a managing director of Seibu Department Stores, the nucleus of the Seibu Saison Group, was appointed president of Osawa. Thus the group successfully added Osawa to its membership, to be used and developed (according to a spokesman) as the group's "foreign trade division."

Another unprofitable company acquired by the Seibu Saison Group was Yoshinoya & Co., the operator and franchiser of Japan's first fast food restaurant chain. Yoshinoya went virtually bankrupt with outstanding debts of over ¥12.6 billion and filed a petition for reorganization in July 1980. With the aid of a similar Seibu Saison commitment, Yoshinoya's reorganization plan was approved by the court and became effective in March 1983, and Mr Seiji Tsutsumi, the Seibu Saison Group's chief executive officer, was appointed as Yoshinoya's receiver. In this way, Yoshinoya became part of the Seibu Saison Group, and successfully paid off its debts within four years.

Negotiations are also reported to be currently in progress between the Seibu Saison Group and the Kurushima Dock

Group, which has been in serious financial difficulty for the past several years, over Seibu's possible purchase of the Kansai Steamship Company, a member of the Kurushima Group and the leading supplier of steamship liner services in the Kansai district, primarily in the Inland Sea area. The proposed purchase is part of a scheme to rescue Kurushima, which currently own 43.7% of Kansai's issued and outstanding common shares. According to the Sumitomo Bank, the Seibu Group, which is already heavily involved in tourism and leisure, is bound to be very interested.

A group of companies, mentioned in Section 2.1(1), the Daiei Group, has recently become very active in acquiring unprofitable companies, or those with accumulated debts. The group is headed by the Daiei Corporation, one of the nation's largest supermarket chain operator. It recently acquired the Riccar Corporation, which was one of the nation's largest manufacturers of sewing machines and which sold its products door-to-door through a unique instalment payment plan. In July 1984, Riccar suffered financial collapse, with outstanding debts of ¥111 billion, and subsequently filed a petition for reorganization: the petition was granted in February 1985. However, reorganization could not be achieved without help from a major industrial group. At the request of the Ministry of International Trade and Industry (MITI), Daiei had taken part in Riccar's reorganization since the filing of the petition, through equity participation in some of Riccar's subsidiaries and other similar measures. In February 1987 Daiei finally announced its intention to acquire the controlling interest in Riccar and then assume full responsibility for implementation of the reorganization plan. With court approval, Daiei is to appoint a trustee to oversee Riccar's business operations and assets. Therefore, Daiei will have acquired a virtually bankrupt company with a deficit of over ¥100 billion, and will have to assume responsibility for part of that huge debt – but the benefits gained will be three-fold.

First, there is Riccar's unique instalment payment plan. A consumer wishing to purchase a Riccar product pays by instalment, with interest, and in so doing defers his purchase until the aggregate amount paid, plus the interest accrued, reaches the then effective purchase price (it is understood that MITI is unwilling to grant any further licenses for schemes of this nature). Daiei extended its operations in 1983 to include a mail-order business, but revenues from mail order remained disappointing, at approximately ¥10 billion a year, only 0.6% of the company's total annual revenue. At the same time, and despite its huge financial resources, the provisions of the Large Retail Stores Restrictions Act virtually prohibited Daiei from opening new supermarkets. But with access to Riccar's door-to-door sales scheme, and assuming that Daiei will remain able to utilize Riccar's license, new prospects immediately open up.

The second, related, benefit is the volume of potential new customers – Riccar's list runs to 700,000 across the entire nation.

Third, the recent land price inflation in and around the Tokyo metropolitan area has meant that Riccar's headquarters and the land around it (approximately 1,200 square meters, in the most expensive business quarter of Tokyo) now has a current market value that is unbelievably high, compared to a relatively low book value.

Recently, Daiei has announced that, at the request of the Mitsubishi Bank, it intends to purchase from the Kurushima Dock Group 60% of the issued and outstanding shares of the Oriental Hotel Company, which was established in 1982 and presently owns and operates the Oriental Hotel in Kobe, one of the nation's oldest Western-style hotels. Kurushima is understood to have decided to part with Oriental to improve liquidity: Daiei already has a foothold in the hotel industry, owning and operating five hotels in major Japanese cities.

Many other similar cases could be cited. For example, in July 1985, the Canon Sales Company, a subsidiary of Canon, acquired a substantial holding (16%) in the Nippon Typewriters

Company. (It is believed that Canon kept its share holding to below 20% in order to avoid being saddled with at least part of Nippon Typewriters' huge deficits which, in accordance with the Equity Method, would have made a visible impression on Canon's financial statements.) Despite the growth in popularity of computerized word processors, Nippon had continued to market manual typewriters, and had become totally unprofitable by May 1985. Canon Sales has been able to gain virtual control, and thus avail itself of Nippon's existing nationwide marketing network, with over 400 salesmen.

In May 1983, Kyoto Ceramic (presently known as Kyocera), which was one of the top blue chip companies, acquired and merged with the Yashica Company, formerly a very successful camera manufacturer. At the time, Yashica was near financial collapse, due primarily to poor merchandising policies.

In 1986 the CSK Corporation, which was one of the nation's largest computer software service companies, acquired the Bell System 24 Company, a provider of telephone call transfer services, in order to rescue the Chescom Group, which had once been a very successful provider of similar services, and of which Bell System 24 was a member, from financial distress.

In October 1986, 100% of the issued and outstanding common shares of the Saitama Silver Seiko Company were acquired by the Plus Corporation, which was one of the nation's largest manufacturers of office supplies and business machines. Seriously affected by the US Government's assessment of anti-dumping duties on its products and by poor US printer sales due to a recession in the US computer industry, and further weakened by the sharp appreciation of the yen, Saitama Silver Seiko was in serious financial difficulties, with an accumulated deficit of nearly ¥300 million. Plus Corporation's primary purpose in making the acquisition is reputed to have been to utilize Saitama Silver Seiko's production facilities.

In October 1986, Uniden Corporation, a manufacturer of communications equipment (perhaps most widely known because of its TV commercials featuring US golfer Jack Nicklaus) acquired 51% of the issued and outstanding common shares of the Weston Corporation, a communications equipment manufacturer listed on the Second Section of the Tokyo Stock Exchange. Uniden had just gone public as an over-the-counter company a month previously, while Weston was in financial trouble at the time because of poor sales of stereo loudspeakers, with huge debts amounting to approximately ¥5.4 billion as of the end of March 1986. The acquisition was largely made possible by the Heiwa Sogo Bank, Weston's largest creditor, which agreed to relieve Weston from its outstanding loan obligations.

In March 1987, the Nippon Steel Corporation acquired the Japacs Corporation, a leading manufacturer of electric spark machines. Japacs was also in financial trouble due to the sharp appreciation of the yen, and problems with defective products. Although Japacs had an operational deficit of over ¥1 billion, Nippon Steel decided to acquire it as part of its diversification program for the "post-steel" era.

Finally, in April 1987, the Asahipen Corporation, a manufacturer of household paints and protective coatings, acquired the Teijin Papirio Company, a cosmetics manufacturer of long standing (established in 1904), as part of its diversification program. At the time, Teijin Papirio's performance was very poor, with an operational deficit of over ¥20 million.

The nature of the transactions by which all these heavily debt-ridden companies were acquired is quite different from the concept of "raiding," and therefore was not subject to adverse social criticism. Indeed, Mr Takami Takahashi, the chairman of Minebea, which has acquired or merged with over 20 companies in Japan since the start of its rapid growth in 1971, has repeatedly stated that "acquisition is a process of reorganization and restructuring."

What is it that makes Japanese corporate management rush in where their American or European counterparts would fear to tread? One of the most important factors is that Japanese shareholders are less critical of management performance. In the US, management ability is always under critical scrutiny by the shareholders, and judgments are often made on the basis of quarterly dividends. On the other hand, Japanese management are typically most concerned with how to preserve jobs for their employees, how to increase their market share, and how to achieve steady growth over the next 10 to 20 years. Japanese shareholders take all this for granted, and are prepared to forgo short-term profitability in the long-term interest, as long as recovery takes no longer than, say, four to five years.

In this connection, one interesting episode is worth noting. When approached by the MOF in connection with the ailing Heiwa Sogo Bank, the Sumitomo Bank, which was known for its powerful resources and aggressive tactics, feigned indifference at first – despite its considerable interest – because it did not want to give the general public the impression that it was an aggressive "raider." As one of Sumitomo's senior executives put it, "What we are trying to achieve is not to step into someone else's garden and pick the flowers growing there."

4.8 ACQUISITION OF PROFITABLE COMPANIES

Not all companies acquired in Japan are necessarily unprofitable or heavily debt-ridden: a few cases do exist in which Japanese corporations have acquired other profitable companies.

For example, in March 1987, as part of its diversification program, Furukawa Co. Ltd acquired the Unic Corporation, a successful and profitable mobile crane manufacturer with 40% of the domestic market. Unic's sales revenue for the year ended March 1986 totalled approximately ¥12.2 billion, out of which it made net earnings of about ¥730 million before tax and other deductions. Unic met no opposition from its employees – traditionally one of the most difficult hurdles to clear. The employees were simply told, only days before the completion of the deal, that there would be a change in ownership but everything else would remain the same: They accepted this calmly.

Another similar case is that of Fontaine Co. Ltd, which was one of the subsidiaries of the Kanegafuchi Chemical Industries Corporation and was the nation's largest manufacturer of wigs and hairpieces for women, with 25% of the domestic market. In 1984, Kanegafuchi sold Fontaine to Aderans Co. Ltd, a leading manufacturer of wigs for men. The sale went through even though Fontaine's performance for the financial year ending 1984 was very satisfactory, with annual sales of over ¥2.47 billion, yielding net earnings before tax and other deductions of ¥130 million. According to one of its senior executives, Kanegafuchi's reasoning was that its new policy was to part with divisions and operations that did not fit in happily with its plans to make best use of its technical and management resources as an integrated chemicals manufacturer – no matter how profitable the division might be. Kanegafuchi was determined to concentrate all of its available resources in promising areas within the chemicals industry; while Aderans regarded Fontaine as an attractive buy because it had concessions in 136 department stores throughout the country, plus six direct sales offices located in major cities.

Kanegafuchi also sold another wholly owned subsidiary in 1984, for the same reason: Nangoku Pulp Co. Ltd, a producer of specialty paper used in the manufacture of teabags, was sold to the Nippon Paper Trading Co. Ltd. Nangoku Pulp was also profitable at the time of the sale.

Although it is not widespread public knowledge, Toshiba is one of the large companies that are actively selling their subsidiaries. In 1979 it sold Toshiba Pharmaceutical Co. Ltd and Toshiba Chemical Industries Co. Ltd to the TDK Corporation. Another subsidiary, Hokko Electronics Co. Ltd, was sold to the

Tokin Corporation in 1982, and this was followed by the sale of the Tajiri Machinery Engineering Co. Ltd to the Unisef Corporation in 1984. According to one of Toshiba's executive vice-presidents, "We think electronic technologies and products for industrial applications are the most promising and important fields for us in the future. Therefore, we will not hesitate to sell those of our subsidiaries and operating divisions which are irrelevant to any of those important fields, no matter how much contribution they are making or are expected to make to our consolidated performance."

The recent history of Kanegafuchi and Toshiba in particular seems to indicate that the attitude of Japanese business executives toward mergers and acquisitions has started to shift significantly. And perhaps the long-established consensus that it is shameful to sell a profitable company, or that to acquire a profitable company might be criticized as "raiding," has already started to break down.

5

A Practical Strategy:
How to Acquire a Japanese
Company

5.1 ECONOMIC STRUCTURES AND BUSINESS
TRADITIONS

In preparing to acquire a Japanese company, it is important to give due consideration to Japan's economic structure and business traditions. In many important respects, Japan's economic and business heritage differs markedly from that of America or Europe.

5.1.1 Who owns corporations?

While in America the chairman of the board or the president of a company addresses his shareholders with the words "your company," in Japan his counterpart invariably refers to "our company." While Americans and Europeans consider the shareholders to be the owners, the Japanese consider that the company belongs to its management and employees – and this is the fundamental difference between the two business cultures. Japanese corporation law is substantially the same as Anglo-American or continental European corporation law: under the law, corporations in Japan are deemed to be owned by their shareholders. But the difference lies in culture or social sentiment. In America, when a company becomes an acquisition target, the management is generally considered to be obliged to act in the best interests of the shareholders; however, Japanese corporate employees tend to regard the prospect of acquisition as "occupation" or "capture." It is very important to understand this fundamental difference.

5.1.2 Approval from the banks

Any foreign investor hoping to acquire a Japanese company must first obtain the approval of one of that company's major shareholders – the major bank or other lending institution. The best course of action is to purchase from that major shareholder its holdings in the target company: if this is not possible, approval should still be sought before purchasing a substantial block of shares on the open market. Although there is no legal requirement, it is important to recognize the role that banks and other lending institutions have traditionally played in Japan, particularly because of their influence over their borrowers, and therefore to "grease the wheels."

In order to gain a better understanding of this role, it is worthwhile to consider the historical pattern of share ownership in Japan: changes in the distribution of share ownership of listed companies from 1949 to 1985 are shown in Figure 5.1.

As the figure clearly shows, the numbers of individual investors and their holdings have decreased steadily since World War II – in 1987 the figure dropped to below 25%. On the other hand, holdings by financial institutions and other corporate investors have increased steadily, reaching 34.5% by 1975 and as much as 39.3% in 1985. In 1986, 58.3% of the largest shareholders of the top 100 listed Japanese companies were banks or other financial institutions ("largest" here is defined in terms of assets, with the exception of banks and other financial institutions themselves). To prevent them from exercising undue

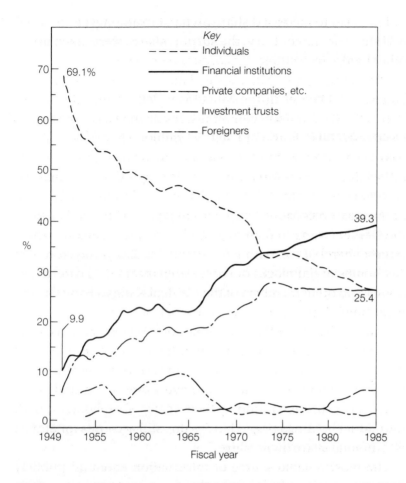

Figure 5.1 Changes in shareholding ratios, as classified by shareholders, FY 1949 to FY 1985: the data for financial institutions exclude investment trusts.

Source: Nihon Keizai Shimbun, July 29, 1986

control over the Japanese economy as a whole, banks and other financial institutions were required by Article 11 of the Anti-monopoly Act, as amended, to divest themselves, by no later than December 1987, of equity ownership in any Japanese company in excess of 5% (or 10% if such a corporation is engaged in the insurance business). However, this restriction did not lead to increased share ownership amongst individual investors: on the contrary, the surplus shares were taken up by other banks, institutions, or corporate investors.

For example, the Mitsubishi Bank was rated as the fifth largest shareholder in the Mitsubishi Petrochemical Co. Ltd, with 5.8% (20.7 million common stock shares) as of the end of December 1986. Forced to sell 2.9 million shares, Mitsubishi sold them directly to other banks and financial institutions, rather than to individual investors through the stock market. Another good example is that of Nippon Columbia Co. Ltd, one of the major recording companies in Japan. At the end of 1986, the Dai-Ichi Kangyo Bank was ranked as the company's third largest shareholder, with 8.6% equity, and was forced to sell 3.6%. Substantial blocks of shares were again sold directly, in this case to other members of the Dai-Ichi Kangyo Bank Group, including Nippon Tochitatemono Co. Ltd.

Thus Article 11 of the Antimonopoly Act (as amended) has failed to bring about an increase in the number of individual investors or in individual share ownership. Ironically, most listed companies in Japan now have more banks and other financial institutions among their major shareholders: with individual holdings pegged to 5% this still accounts for almost 50% of total share ownership.

The most reliable source of information about all publicly held corporations in Japan is the *Company Handbook*, a very popular quarterly published by the Toyo Economic Publishing Company. It is available in both Japanese and English editions.

Japanese banks and other financial institutions are eager to maintain equity participation in other companies in order to establish "more than average" business relations and/or direct channels of communication, but not to seek capital gains or investment income. It is common practice for a Japanese commercial bank to buy a small share holding in a particular company to encourage that company to become a new client, or in the hope of becoming the company's major lender. This tactic is often successful, and Japanese companies normally welcome a small equity participation of this kind. However, they would certainly not welcome the bank's active involvement in company management: all that they expect is "untied" financial assistance, from an important group of stable, friendly, and silent stockholders. In fact, it is extremely rare for banks to attend and put forward propositions at shareholders' meetings. Their normal practice is simply to sign and return the proxy cards distributed in advance of such meetings.

According to 1985 statistics, the Nippon Mutual Life Assurance Company (Nissei), one of the nation's largest financial institutions, was the largest stockholder of 69 of 1,806 listed companies, and was the second to fifth largest stockholder of a further 432 listed companies. Yet it has remained a friendly silent stockholder: no instances have been publicly reported in which it has sent representatives to company meetings or refused to grant proxies solicited by company management. As Mr Tokutaro Hirose, the executive vice-president of Nissei, said in a recent press interview: "We do not want to actively participate in the personnel administration of any other company in which we are a stockholder or to help someone acquire it." In a 1986 press interview, Mr Masaaki Sugishita, manager of the Industrial Bank of Japan's funds department, reinforced the traditional viewpoint: "Banks' current equity positions in other companies and firms represent friendly business relations which have taken so many good years to establish that they cannot be changed in a day."

5.1.3 Becoming the largest stockholder

In the first instance, acquiring companies should consider that they have achieved success if they can obtain enough shares to become the target company's largest stockholder, rather than trying to obtain a majority interest at once. It is a logical consequence of the current ownership structure in Japan that ownership and management are so widely separated from each other that current management teams, with the passive support of their silent stockholders, can remain in a *de facto* controlling position for as long as they want unless, of course, they commit serious errors. The "largest stockholder" status gives a foreign investor enough influence to participate actively and effectively in the company's management, but it is often unwise – or even harmful – to set out with the ultimate objective of acquisition of a majority interest. In fact, in most cases involving only Japanese companies, the acquiring company has stopped purchasing shares, in the expectation that it has successfully acquired the target company, at an ownership level of only 10–20%.

Consider the acquisition by Toyota Motors of Hamamatsu Photonics, a successful R & D oriented venture business specializing in state-of-the-art optoelectronic technology, and manufacturing infrared and ultraviolet TV cameras, and ultra-high-speed photometric devices. Hamamatsu's net profit for 1986, before tax and other deductions, was ¥540 million. Toyota, which had become known as one of the very few large companies that seemed to have no interest in mergers and acquisitions, suddenly became very active, making a series of acquisitions that included a block of two million Hamamatsu common shares; this purchase cost ¥3.8 billion, but represented only 8.1% of Hamamatsu's issued and outstanding shares. Toyota became the second largest stockholder: the largest shareholder was the Photonics Stock Ownership Association, the nominee for Hamamatsu's employee stock ownership plan, which owned 17.1%. "Though Toyota will provide Hamamatsu Photonics with as much financial assistance as needed," said one Toyota executive in a press interview, "we have no intention of actively participating in its management." Toyota is said to have decided upon this level of stock ownership out of respect because they wanted to "pay due respect to and maintain the impetus which made Hamamatsu Photonics grow, namely, its employees' strong belief that they owned and controlled the company."

Toyota subsequently acquired the Sanritsu Automation Co. Ltd, a Tokyo-based venture business with a share capital of ¥27.3 million, and having proprietary know-how in the field of microcomputer-based automation control systems. In late August 1987, Toyota purchased an additional 23,400 Sanritsu common shares for approximately ¥200 million. Toyota then became Sanritsu's largest shareholder, but its ownership in Sanritsu remained at 30%, with only a couple of (part-time) seats on Sanritsu's board of directors. American and European potential investors should take note that even an industrial giant such as Toyota is prepared to tread gently, and acquire no more than "largest shareholder" status, even when the target company is only a relatively small venture business.

Many other similar cases of recent acquisitions in Japan can be cited, such as the acquisition by Nippon Cement of the ADS Company, a Nara-based manufacturer of image processing devices. In this case, Nippon Cement only acquired less than 5% of ADS's common shares. Dai-Ichi Seiko acquired a 27.8% ownership of Nissho Guiken, an Urawa-based R & D oriented company specializing in the development of new photo-electronic products; while the Taisei Corporation acquired a 30% ownership of Sigario Japan, a Tokyo-based R & D oriented company specializing in the development of innovative food products using brown rice powder.

The Ajinomoto Corporation, one of the nation's leading manufacturers of food and pharmaceutical products, is another acquisition-conscious company. "The primary objective of mergers and acquisitions, as we see it," says Mr Tadao Suzuki, executive vice-president of Ajinomoto, "should be to establish friendly business relations between the acquiring company and the target company, and to put their financial, engineering, and human resources together for their mutual benefit through friendly negotiations." On the basis of this M & A policy, in

October 1985 Ajinomoto peaceably acquired 20% of the outstanding common shares of Shimadaya Honten Co. Ltd of Tokyo, one of the nation's largest noodle producers, and also acquired the right to appoint members of Shimadaya Honten's board of directors.

In October 1986, Nisshin Oil Mills Ltd acquired the Kobayashi Pharmaceutical Industry Co. Ltd, a Tokyo-based company with a share capital of ¥130 million. In this case, however, Nisshin only acquired 26.67% of Kobayashi's outstanding common shares through a negotiated third-party allotment. A business cooperation arrangement was simultaneously drawn up between the two companies, for the purpose of promoting joint research, production, and marketing. Under this arrangement the two companies are making joint efforts to develop new medicines to combat conditions such as arteriosclerosis and senile dementia. As part of the program, Nisshin now has two of its senior executives on the Kobayashi board of directors.

The Asahi Glass Corporation, one of Japan's largest glass manufacturers, decided in 1984 to expand its lines of business to include the manufacturing and marketing of electronic products, through the acquisition of two public corporations listed on the Second Section of the Tokyo Stock Exchange and on another stock exchange. Asahi used its banks (including securities firms) as intermediaries to locate suitable companies. With this assistance, Asahi successfully acquired a 13.5% ownership of Nippon Carbide Industries Co., Inc., and a 26.3% ownership of Elna Co. Ltd, in each instance becoming the largest shareholder. According to a reliable source, Asahi purchased its 26.3% stake in Elna from the previous largest shareholder, the General Corporation, for approximately ¥3.0 billion, or ¥550 per share (based on the average closing price of Elna shares on the Tokyo Stock Exchange during the month prior to completion of the transaction). Asahi is reputed to have decided against a majority ownership in Elna, in order to assure the management team, officers, and employees of their continued independence. This course of action also ensured that Asahi would not meet any opposition from Elna's employee labor union, or from customers or suppliers. From Asahi's point of view, the 26.3% stake was, as a senior executive put it, "enough percentage ownership for Asahi to have and exercise effective control over the management of Elna and to discourage the other major shareholders of Elna from interfering with the exchange of technologies and know-how between Asahi and Elna."

These examples reinforce the fact that, in Japan, even minority share ownership can bring with it virtual control over the management of the target company.

The 1987 purchases of Suido Kiko Co. Ltd and Nippon Eternit Pipe by Misawa Homes have already been discussed in Section 2.4.2. Misawa obtained a 19.6% holding in Suido Kiko (a company with a share capital of ¥650 million), and in February it purchased 7.66 million common shares of Nippon Eternit Pipe from Nippon Cement, establishing 35.3% ownership. Using its influence as largest shareholder, Misawa has entered into a business arrangement with Suido Kiko in the field of household plumbing systems, and is now also pushing Nippon Eternit Pipe to expand its lines of business to include the construction and operation of resort, athletic, and leisure facilities. It is said that the price of Suido Kiko shares was fixed at ¥1,200 per share – following the advice of Cosmo Securities Co. Ltd, which acted as mediator for Misawa – and that Misawa paid ¥2,844 million for its 19.6% stake. Misawa is said to have paid approximately ¥5.0 billion for its 35.3% stake in Nippon Eternit Pipe.

In November 1987, SECOM Co. Ltd, Japan's largest security service company, acquired the Hochiki Co. Ltd, the second largest fire alarm manufacturer, whose common shares were listed on the First Section of the Tokyo Stock Exchange. Again, SECOM acquired only a 20% stake in Hochiki, becoming its largest shareholder. Before this, SECOM had successfully acquired Nohmi Bosai Kogyo Co. Ltd, the nation's largest fire alarm manufacturer, whose common shares were listed on the Second Section at Tokyo, by purchasing 25% ownership to become Nohmi Bosai's largest shareholder. Following the acquisition of Hochiki, SECOM announced that it was going to promote a joint R & D program between Hochiki and Nohmi Bosai to develop new fire alarm and security systems, for homes and for large commercial buildings. SECOM now has effective control over the two largest manufacturers in this sector, with a combined market share in excess of 50%.

Mr Yoshihiko Miyauchi, president of Orient Leasing Co. Ltd, which has been very keen on mergers and acquisitions for the purpose of diversification, states his company's acquisitions policy as follows:

It would be a very wearisome thing to acquire other companies through hostile acquisition and then manage these companies, while having a difficult time with their existing management teams. Therefore, generally we are not interested in hostile mergers or acquisitions. I know that in America the most important factor to consider in determining whether your company should acquire another company or not, or whether you should recommend that shareholders accept an acquisition offer, is the nature and extent of the merit that would be brought to the shareholders. But in Japan we do not think that way.

Orient Leasing acquired Osaka Ichioka Co. Ltd, an Osaka-based realty company, in 1986. However, its ownership was limited to 26% and it had no representation on Osaka Ichioka's board, except that one of Osaka Ichioka's statutory auditors was Orient Leasing's appointee (see also Section 5.8.1).

5.1.4 A first approach: Mutually profitable tie-ups

In the light of the resentment and outright difficulty – not to mention complete failure – that an attempt at a hostile acquisition would undoubtedly bring about, a good first approach is to offer a mutually profitable business arrangement, or a program such as cross-licensing, a distributorship, or joint R & D. This makes the acquisition scheme as palatable as possible to the Japanese target company.

As mentioned earlier, most successful cases involving Japanese individuals and corporations have started in this way, as the following two examples demonstrate.

In September 1987, Mitsubishi Chemicals acquired eight million additional common shares in Tokyo Tanabe Pharmaceutical, through private placement, becoming Tokyo Tanabe's largest shareholder, with a total holding of 12 million common shares. Behind this acquisition lay a mutually profitable business arrangement: on the one hand, Mitsubishi Chemicals expanded its sales outlets for pharmaceutical products, and on the other Tokyo Tanabe was seen to expand its product range.

JUSCO, one of Japan's largest supermarket chains, acquired a 9% stake in Chuyu, a fast food chain operator, through the purchase of one million common shares, again through private placement, and became Chuyu's third largest shareholder. JUSCO then entered into a cooperative arrangement with Chuyu: while Chuyu owned some attractive vacant sites, on which it could not make any profit, JUSCO was having difficulty in securing prime sites on which it could build further supermarkets – the arrangement enabled the resources to meet the needs!

As demonstrated by the above examples, business tie-ups and equity participation often go hand-in-hand, to endorse the mutual commitment of both parties, and the arrangement often takes the form of a package deal. The best approach, therefore, is to start by suggesting a suitable tie-up, without making any mention of equity participation at all – this will soon be offered by the other party in return.

5.1.5 Mutual equity participation as a "tranquilizer"

In November 1987, Morinaga Co. Ltd, the nation's largest confectionery firm, entered into a business cooperation arrangement with Fujiya Co. Ltd, a leading confectionery firm, primarily with a view to promoting joint purchasing of raw materials and joint overseas ventures. At the same time, each acquired equity in the other: Morinaga purchased 3.6% ownership of Fujiya, and Fujiya 2.26% ownership of Morinaga, each becoming the fifth largest shareholder of the other (and the top nonbank or noninsurance-company shareholder). An intercompany committee, the Cooperation Promotion Committee, consisting of board members and senior management from both companies, was formed to actively pursue the objectives of the arrangement. This mutual cooperation, with mutual equity participation, does look far more acceptable to Japanese corporate society than a threatening offer of outright acquisition.

5.1.6 Management teams and boards of directors

As has been emphasized earlier, a stable environment is very important, and any feeling of "raiding" or "occupation" must be avoided at all costs. From this point of view, it is not always desirable to vote out or remove a large number of the members of the current management team of an acquired company in the aftermath of acquisition, nor to ask for too many seats on the board of directors. To act otherwise would be to invite noncooperation from managers, employees, customers, suppliers, and banks alike; noncooperation that could make it extremely difficult to operate the business as before.

Toyo Sash, which acquired Nittetsu Curtain Walls in 1985, seconded only one executive to Nittetsu, making one appointment to Nittetsu's board in order to reorganize and improve the company's ailing manufacturing and marketing divisions. That one individual carried sole responsibility for the task, as well as planning and implementing programs to curtail production costs. Similarly, only one person was newly appointed to the board of Nittetsu Sash Sales, acquired at the same time. He did a remarkable job of discreetly and successfully persuading as many as 85% of Nittetsu's distributors and subdistributors to convert to Toyo products! "One of the most important keys to this successful conversion," he said later, "was that I have been repeatedly told by my boss and kept telling myself that if we give the employees, suppliers and/or customers of Nittetsu even the slightest impression that we are the occupation force with the power to control their future, we would fail and all our efforts would become meaningless." This is why Toyo kept transfers of personnel to Nittetsu to the absolute minimum.

Minebea adopts a similar policy: when it acquires another company it usually seconds only one person – often an accounting expert. For example when, in May 1978, it acquired Hokuto Audio Engineering, an unprofitable designer and manufacturer of audio loudspeakers, only one person, an accounting expert, was seconded to the Hokuto board. He took sole charge of planning and implementing cost reduction and budget control programs to restore Hokuto's profitability. As one of Minebea's senior executives says, "If you send one of your people to a company you acquire as a member of its board, you should tell him to devote himself fully as a player of inconspicuous roles, so that the officers and employees of the company do not feel uneasy or uncomfortable."

The principle of being cautious about making sweeping changes in management or in the boardroom is not always observed in Japan. If an acquiring company is fortunate enough to gain a virtual, or absolute, majority interest in a target company in a friendly manner, then little hesitation may be shown. For example, Orient Leasing was able to acquire 46.5% ownership of Toshiki Co. Ltd, one of the nation's leading carpet manufacturers, the common shares of which were listed on the Second Section of the Tokyo Stock Exchange, and 58% ownership of Akane Securities Co. Ltd – in both cases it unhesitatingly replaced the presidents of the acquired companies with its own appointees. But rapid replacement is still rare: few Japanese acquiring companies venture to replace presidents of target companies immediately after acquisition, unless there is some unavoidable reason to do so. Even when such a reason exists, it is not uncommon for a new appointee to be a neutral candidate, such as a retired officer from one of the acquired company's banks, rather than one of their own officers or directors. This minimizes the risk of the "occupying force" syndrome.

5.1.7 Labor union cooperation

In Japan, labor unions are generally not trade unions. In most cases, a labor union represents the employees of only one company. Therefore, unlike their counterparts in the US and Europe, labor unions in Japan tend to have a rather strong affinity with the companies of which their members are employees – and the cooperation of the unions can be vital.

The following is an interesting example, involving the Okuma Machinery Works, a 90-year-old industrial machinery manufacturer, and one of Japan's leading producers of numerically controlled lathes. Okuma is a public company, the shares of which are listed on the First Section of the Tokyo Stock Exchange. In January 1988, the president of Okuma, Mr Takeo Okuma, decided to appoint his eldest son, Hajime Okuma, who was then one of the company's vice-presidents, as his successor. But the labor union was severely critical, complaining that Okuma was a public company, and therefore not family property – the union wanted both men to resign. Under the law, only the shareholders have the right to appoint or dismiss the president; nevertheless, the union continued to press its case. The confrontation was finally settled through the mediation of the Tokai Bank, Okuma's major lender, by the replacement of

Mr Takeo Okuma as president of the company with one of the bank's executive vice-presidents. In other words, the labor union succeeded in removing the company president from office.

Labor unions are strong adversaries, and the success of mergers and acquisitions can depend very much on the degree of cooperation that can be achieved with them – as can the future performance of the company. It is widely believed that the Sumitomo Bank's recent failure to acquire the Kansai Sogo Bank was due, at least in part, to strong union opposition. And Minebea, which already had a 19% stake in Sankyo Seiki, felt it necessary to mail pleas for support and cooperation directly to Sankyo Seiki employees, in a bid to make that attempted acquisition a success.

5.1.8 The relative importance of the price factor

In Japan, the acquisition price is not the key to success or failure, although it remains an important factor. As mentioned earlier, most Japanese business executives and owners regard acquisition as a matter of dishonor, and even if they are prepared to sell they are not overly concerned with how much money they can make. They are more concerned with justifying themselves, and saving face when selling to someone whom they do not know well. There is a corollary: if the acquiring party can offer something which will contribute to face-saving or personal justification, the sense of relief may well make it more likely that the owner or chief executive will be prepared to part with his company or business. It is true to say that Japanese owners and chief executive officers often react very slowly to acquisition offers, because they need time to resolve this face-saving or justification problem to their own satisfaction before they proceed. Once the problem is resolved, they proceed rather quickly. Japanese owners and chief executive officers are so emotional and sentimental that, in general, financial terms and conditions alone – no matter how attractive – are insufficient to persuade them to accept an offer. If American or European potential investors try to provide further financial incentives, such as a higher acquisition price or extravagant retirement benefits, while the owner or chief executive officer is still trying to resolve his personal dilemma, this can actually exacerbate the process and cause further delay.

One of the owner's major concerns is often that key employees and senior officers, who may have worked for the company for 40 to 50 years, may criticize him bitterly for betraying them in order to obtain personal capital gains. This must be avoided at all costs and, in extreme cases, can frustrate the entire acquisition effort.

In America and Europe, the acquisition price is generally evaluated by the discounted cashflow method, in which the market value of the target company is determined by the current value of the expected cashflow of the company over a certain future period, using an appropriate discount rate. However, this method is not generally accepted in Japan. In the discounted cashflow method, the future cashflow of the company must be estimated correctly: this depends on future prospects and trading conditions, and inevitably involves considerable subjectivity, to which the Japanese object.

In Japan, the acquisition value of a privately held company is usually determined by its book value (shareholders' equity) adjusted upward on the basis of the goodwill and the difference between the book and market values of any land owned by the company. In other words, it is determined on the basis of the most recent company balance sheet. The total liabilities are subtracted from the total assets as shown on the balance sheet. The market price of land is usually determined by an impartial licensed real-estate appraiser, while the value of the goodwill is determined by mutual negotiation between the two parties to the acquisition.

5.2 THE ROLE OF THE BANK

The role of the bank as adviser is important, and it is equally important to take advantage of the "main bank" system, and the close relationship that exists between the main bank and the target company.

While in America and Europe investment banks play an important part in mergers and acquisitions, they have no Japanese counterparts. In recent times, the major commercial banks that act as the "main banks" of the target companies have taken on this role. To qualify as the "main bank" of a Japanese company, a bank must usually carry out the following functions:

1 It must be the largest lender to the company.
2 It must have a long-lasting business relationship with the company, its subsidiaries, and affiliated companies, not only in the lending business but also in deposits, foreign exchange, and custodian or trustee service businesses.
3 It must be one of the major shareholders in the company.
4 It must have one or more seats on the board of directors or the board of statutory auditors of the company.
5 It must have committed itself to the company's funding operations so extensively as to be able to readily agree to extend the due date of any outstanding loan and/or extend additional loan finance to the company if necessary.
6 It must maintain such a close business relationship with the company as to permit it to act as lead manager in the case of a syndicated loan to the company.

The existence of an equity relation between the bank and the company is very important: all listed companies in Japan have banks among their major shareholders. As to management participation, the great majority of listed and major nonlisted companies in Japan have bank executives on their boards of directors or statutory auditors.

For example, at the end of 1985 most of the major commercial banks had representation on the boards of directors or statutory auditors of the following major listed companies:

1 The Dai-Ichi Kangyo Bank: Hazama Gumi, Teikoku Chemical Engineering, Orient Finance, Daikyo Kanko, and Shibusawa Warehouses.

2 The Mitsubishi Bank: Takasago, Torikoshi Flour Mills, Osaka Oxygen, Mochida Pharmaceutical, Daido Concrete, Hirano Metals, Daiwa Reiki, Akai, Matsuya, the Aomuri Bank, Diamond Leasing, and SECOM.

3 The Fuji Bank: Matsui Construction, Takasago, Sakurada Machinery, Teikoku Piston Rings, Oki Electric, Takara, Okura Trading, Uni Charm, Jujiya, Chujitsuya, and LIFE.

4 The Sumitomo Bank: Sumitomo Coal Mining, Kajima Construction, Sumitomo Construction, Daiwa Housing, Asahi Breweries, Kawashima Textile, Taisho Pharmaceutical, Ishii Iron Works, Sanoyas, Descent, Moonbat, Ryosan, the Shiga Sogo Bank, Osaka Buildings, and Sumitomo Real Estate.

Other major commercial banks, including the Sanwa, Tokai, and Taiyo Kobe Banks had similar representation.

There have been numerous cases in which commercial banks have played a dominant role in rescuing and reorganizing major companies that were experiencing serious financial difficulties. For example, the Mitsubishi Bank played a major role in the reorganization of the Akai Company, as did the Sumitomo Bank in the case of Mazda Motors and Asahi Breweries. The decisive role played by the Tokai Bank in resolving the dispute between Okuma's management and labor union provides yet another example (see Section 5.1.7).

American and European potential investors should not disregard or underestimate the strong influence that Japanese commercial banks have, over not only the financial but also the managerial affairs of the companies of which they are the main banks. In order to complete a successful acquisition, it is essential to maintain close contact with the target company's main bank. Its approval should be sought first: if it is not readily forthcoming then at least it should be in a position in which it is unlikely to turn against the proposed acquisition. If either overt or covert support can be obtained from the main bank, then a successful acquisition will almost certainly be secured.

In the case of Akai, for example, the Mitsubishi Bank, in close cooperation with another member of the Mitsubishi Group, Mitsubishi Electric, offered positive support – both financial and otherwise – to Akai to rescue it from financial difficulty. The Mitsubishi Bank made additional loans, seconded one of its senior executives to be Akai's new president, and arranged to sell some of Akai's factories to a real-estate company, which was also a member of the Mitsubishi Group, to improve Akai's liquidity. The bank's free hand in Akai's reorganization would have made it very easy for an American or European corporation that wanted to acquire a Japanese electric and electronic firm, and that had somehow learned that Akai was about to sell some of its factories, to step in and make an acquisition. In approaching the bank, it would of course be best if the acquiring company were to convey the impression that it wished to make its purchase in order to help the bank perform the rescue operation.

Major Japanese commercial banks have recently been eager to expand their services to include investment banking. For example, the Mitsubishi Bank has recently organized a new operating group, the Information Development Group, to render advisory and consulting services in the M & A field (this is the bank's seventh operating group). Other major commercial banks have followed suit, but there is a snag. Banks are not officially permitted by the MOF to engage in the M & A related advisory and consulting business. At present, the ministry appears to be turning a blind eye to the banks' activities, but the banks are unable to actively promote or publicize their services.

5.3 SECURITIES COMPANIES AS INVESTMENT ADVISERS

Major Japanese securities firms – including the "Big Four," Nomura, Daiwa, Nikko, and Yamaichi – are now very actively rendering M & A consulting and advisory services, and are very keen to improve their resources in this field. In particular, Yamaichi, the forerunner in this respect, began to strengthen its investment banking department as early as 1973. Since then, it has acted as adviser and consultant in a number of mergers and acquisitions, most of which have involved Japanese parties only.

5.4 THE ROLE OF LAWYERS, ACCOUNTANTS, AND CONSULTANTS

5.4.1 Lawyers and acquisitions in Japan

An overview of the situation regarding lawyers in Japan is appropriate before considering their role in acquisitions. The system of legal practice in Japan is entirely different from that of the US, and the term "lawyer" has a very different definition. While in the US most of the 60–70% of law school graduates who successfully pass their bar examinations each year become practising lawyers, in Japan only 0.1% of university law graduates do so, the remaining 99.9% finding employment in corporations, or in national or local government.

This difference stems primarily from the bar examination systems themselves. In Japan, the examinations are so exacting that the pass rate is only 2%. Statistics show that the average age of successful candidates is 29, and that, on average, they have attempted the examination seven times before passing. Once they are successfully through, they are qualified – after state-administered training – to practise whichever branch of law they choose, as judges or public prosecutors (subject to appointment), or as practising attorneys. The "state-adminis-trated training" is a course at the legal training institute run by the Supreme Court: this two-year apprenticeship is a pre-requisite to practising law itself. The course consists of eight months of classes at the institute, followed by 16 months of practical "work experience" in public prosecutors' offices, courts, and law firms. During this time apprentices are paid by the government, as public servants. Because of the Japanese government's huge financial deficits, similar to those of the US government, there is little likelihood that the budget for the legal training institute will increase in the foreseeable future. This budgetary restriction places severe constraints on the number of legal apprentices accepted by the institute each year: the number is limited to 400 or so, of whom about 100 become either judges or public prosecutors, while the remaining 300 become practising attorneys – the latter figure being about 100 times less than that in the US.

Unlike their American counterparts, Japanese lawyers devote most of their time and effort to litigation work: there may be fewer than ten lawyers in Japan who specialize in mergers and acquisitions. However, reflecting the recent level of interest, the numbers have somehow begun to increase stead-ily. Since the number of hostile acquisition cases, although still small, is expected to increase in future, lawyers will increasing-ly be expected to play a more important role in such cases, just as their American counterparts do. Although no law firms devoted solely to mergers and acquisitions presently exist in Japan, it is entirely possible that this may come about in the future.

5.4.2 The invaluable role of accountants

In Japan, the role that certified public accountants (CPAs) play in mergers and acquisitions is very similar to that played by their American counterparts. The most important aspect is the evaluation of the target company, and the provision of consulting services in relation to the tax implications of the transaction.

In Japan there are several methods that can be used to evaluate a target company or its shares. If the target company is listed, the market value of its shares basically determines the value of the company. However, if it is unlisted there are several alternative formulae from which CPAs can choose:

1 the "model for each industry" formula;
2 the dividend income capitalization formula;
3 the net assets value formula;
4 the earning power capitalization formula; and
5 the "compare with previous transactions" formula.

In addition to these, two other methods are commonly used. The first is the method developed by the National Taxation Bureau for inheritance tax purposes, which is described in an official bureau circular entitled *Sozokuzei zaisan hyoka ni kansura kihon tsutatsu* (Basic circular regarding the evaluation of estates). The second is the *kabushiki kokai kakaku santei kijun ni kansura moshiawase* (agreement on the basis of the determination of the public offering price of shares not previously offered to the public), which has been established and accepted by securities firms as a way of determining the offering price of shares when a company goes public.

In actual M & A transactions, CPAs usually determine the fair value of the target company on the basis of professional judgement, taking all the above methods into consideration.

A brief review of the tax implications of the acquisition of Japanese companies now follows, because they are often a key to successful friendly acquisitions of Japanese firms by overseas investors.

Consider a shareholder of a privately owned company who, at some time during the previous three tax years owned 30% or more, and at some point sold 15% or more, of the then issued and outstanding shares of the company. If, within the current

110

tax year, he sells what now amounts to 5% or more of the presently issued and outstanding shares, he becomes liable for capital gains tax. For the purposes of the 30% threshold, any shares in the company that are beneficially held by his "relatives or affiliates" (as defined in the Income Tax Act, as amended) will be considered to be beneficially held by him (see also Section 7.3.1).

To avoid this liability, if the owner of such a company should wish to sell his controlling interest, his best course of action is to sell 14.9% (in each case, percentages refer to the then issued and outstanding shares) in the first year, and thereafter sell 4.9% in each subsequent tax year, until the purchaser acquires the controlling interest. However, this might not suit the purchaser at all, because the process could take years. One way of avoiding this is for the target company to issue shares to the purchaser so that the owner's holding is reduced to below 30%, thus avoiding the threshold problem. Another is for the target and purchasing companies to be merged in a tax-free share-for-share merger, an option which works very well when the merging company is listed.

To obtain an ideal solution, the advice of the CPA is always essential.

5.4.3 Mergers and acquisitions consultants

It used to be the case in Japan that consulting services in relation to mergers and acquisitions could only be provided by the investment banking divisions of commercial banks or securities firms. Recently, however, several specialized firms – albeit small ones – have emerged to provide consulting, brokerage, and intermediary services; some of these firms have been set up and are being managed by people with previous banking/securities experience. Several firms have been set up specifically to act as brokers in the sale and purchase of companies. Interestingly, several of these new firms are trading on the basis of open competitive bidding. In addition, quite a few management consultancy firms, traditionally providers of consulting services in the fields of rationalization and the improvement of management and productivity, are now trying to break into mergers and acquisitions. These firms are relatively good at identifying suitable target companies, and at predicting and analysing the possible effects of transactions on their clients. Another group of firms have diversified from management consultancy in the health-care industry to providing intermediary and brokerage services relating to the sale and purchase of hospitals.

5.5 THE ROLE OF ARBITRAGEURS IN JAPAN

Arbitrageurs exist in Japan, but they differ somewhat from their American counterparts. In the US, when a tender offer is made for a public company by a third party, an arbitrageur will sometimes try to purchase as many shares of the company as possible, for resale to it at a profit. On the other hand, Japanese arbitrageurs are by definition investors who purchase a substantial number of shares in a given company, whether or not at the request of that company's management, for resale to a specific purchaser or purchasers, who may be designated (i) by the company's management, (ii) by the principal for which they are working, or (iii) may be of their own choice. In purchasing a substantial number of shares in a company, they never lose sight of the fact that, if they are unable to sell them at an acceptable price, they will probably be able to persuade the particular company itself to buy them. However, as explained in Section 2.2, the Commercial Code of Japan expressly prohibits corporations organized under its terms of reference from acquiring or holding their own shares, except in certain special circumstances. Therefore a company that is under pressure to purchase its own shares from an arbitrageur has to arrange for its subsidiaries or affiliated companies to make the purchase on its behalf. Arbitrageurs have recently been very active in Japan, as the following examples show.

In 1985 a very powerful group of arbitrageurs, the Videosellers Group, suddenly appeared on the mergers and acquisitions scene in Japan. In April of that year, the group purchased 17.2% of the issued and outstanding common shares of the Fujita Tourist Company which, among other resort facilities, owned and operated Chinzanso, a famous restaurant with a beautiful Japanese-style garden, and the Washington Hotel, both of which are located in central Tokyo. The group subsequently resold its entire holding in Fujita to the Tokyu Corporation, a railway operator and real-estate developer based in the western part of the Tokyo metropolitan area. The Tokyu Corporation is the top company in the Tokyu Group, which consists of 316 companies. Its president, Mr Noboru Gotoh, is the son of the late Mr Keita Gotoh, founder of the Tokyu Group and at one time chairman of the Japan Chamber of Commerce and Industry. In this transaction, the late Mr Kenji Osano, one of the most influential figures in Japan and owner of Kokusai Kogyo Corporation, acted as finder and broker. When it purchased the 17.2% interest in Fujita Tourist from the Videosellers Group, the Tokyu Corporation forced Fujita's management to cooperate fully: after strong initial opposition, Fujita eventually surrendered. Although its primary business up to that time had been the production and marketing of video products, the Videosellers Group was said to have paid almost ¥10 billion to purchase the Fujita shares (at a weighted average of ¥650 per share); it was then said to have earned a capital gain of somewhere between ¥3 billion and ¥4 billion, by selling the shares at a (weighted average) price of ¥920 per share. Funds with which to accomplish this transaction were said to have been raised from a number of financial institutions, some large and some small, and from individual investors.

The Videosellers Group subsequently purchased almost 50% of the issued and outstanding common shares of Fujiya Co. Ltd, one of Japan's leading confectioners: this amounted to approximately 60 million shares. Fuelled by this attempt to corner the market, the price of Fujiya stock – which had previously remained at a level of ¥600 to ¥700 – suddenly became so volatile after the spring of 1985 that it hit a record high of ¥3,370 on the Tokyo Stock Exchange in early 1986. Fearing that the Videosellers Group might sell its shares to some major American food company, Fujiya, its sympathetic shareholders, and its subsidiaries finally agreed to purchase Videosellers' entire holding.

The Kurosawa Group is another, similar group of arbitrageurs. It is headed by the owner of a certain musical instruments shop in Ikebukuro, Tokyo, and is best known for its purchase of a substantial number of common shares in Hamano Industries and Toyo Bosuifu, and their subsequent resale to Misawa Homes (see Section 2.4.2).

The Azabu Group, led by Tokyo-based Azabu Motors Co. Ltd, under the chairmanship of Mr Kitaro Watanabe, is engaged primarily in real estate: it owns valuable tracts of land in the Azabu area, one of Tokyo's most exclusive residential districts. The group is also known for its active trading on the stock market as an arbitrageur. In 1987, Azabu acquired 43% of the issued and outstanding shares of the common stock of 3S Shinwa Corporation, a Tokyo-based trucking and warehousing company, whose shares were listed on the Second Section of the Tokyo Stock Exchange. Subsequently, in July 1988, it acquired a similar, 42% stake in the Tokyo-based Chitose Electrical Construction Co. Ltd, whose shares were also listed on the Second Section. Chitose's major customers were local Japan Railways (JR) companies, which had been set up as a result of the divestiture and division of the former Japan National Railways Corporation.

In both cases, Azabu demanded and obtained only one seat on the acquired company's board of directors, with Mr Watanabe serving as a temporary director and adviser. In the same month, Azabu suddenly sold its entire holding in Tensho Elec-

Table 5.1 Companies in danger of being reclassified on the TSE because of "stock distribution" problems. The table shows the number of stockholders required in each case to prevent reclassification from the First Section to the Second Section.[a]

Company	Number of shareholders required (persons)	Number of one-unit shareholders (persons)	Shortage (persons)
Nippon Eternit Pipe Co. Ltd	2,000	1,821	−179
Nippon Hume Pipe Co. Ltd	2,000	1,632	−368
Janome Sewing Machine Co. Ltd	3,300	1,695	−1,605
Kawatetsu Trading Co. Ltd	2,800	2,362	−438
Nihon Housing Finance Co. Ltd	2,600	2,227	−373
Kokusai Aerial Survey Co.	2,000	1,188	−812
KEIHIN	2,400	2,286	−114
Nippon Television Network Corp.	2,800	2,346	−454

Note:
[a] In each case, the fiscal term to be examined is to the end of March 1988, and the corresponding period of grace extends to the end of March 1989.
Source: Shukan Diamond, July 23, 1988

tric Industries Co. Ltd, a middle-sized Tokyo-based manufacturer of plastic moldings, whose shares were listed on the Second Section at Tokyo, to Orient Leasing Co. Ltd. The holding (5 million shares, acquired by Azabu on the stock market) represented 38% of Tensho's issued and outstanding common shares. Therefore, Orient Leasing, which had already acquired three listed companies (Akane Securities, Toshiki, and Osaka Ichioka), successfully acquired Tensho, through the Azabu Group, at a stroke.

As shown in Table 5.1, the trading behavior of arbitrageurs on the stock market has recently been so aggressive that several listed companies are now in danger of being delisted, because so many of their shares have been locked up by arbitrageurs that the companies are finding it difficult to comply with the

Table 5.2 Companies in danger of being delisted on the TSE because of "stock distribution" problems. The table shows the number of stockholders required in each case to prevent delisting.[a]

Company	Number of shareholders required (persons)	Number of one-unit shareholders (persons)	Shortage (persons)
Janome Sewing Machine Co. Ltd	2,000	1,695	−305
Saibo	750	719	−31
New Tachikawa Aircraft Co. Ltd	750	628	−122
Nihon Regulator Co. Ltd	750	558	−192
Amatsu Steel Ball Mfg. Co. Ltd	1,000	880	−120
Fujitsu Denso	750	673	−77
Mitsui Wharf Co. Ltd	750	630	−120

Note:
[a] In each case, the fiscal term to be examined is to the end of March 1988, and the corresponding period of grace extends to the end of March 1989.
Source: Shukan Diamond, July 23, 1988

Table 5.3 Companies which entered a period of grace before the expiration of the fiscal term ending March 1988

Company	Fiscal term to be examined	Termination of period of grace	Number of shareholders required (persons)	Number of one-unit shareholders (persons)	Shortage (persons)
Fujii	To end Sept. 1987	End Sept. 1988	1,100	1,023	−77
Seirei Industry Co. Ltd	To Nov. 20, 1987	End Nov. 1988	1,100	896	−204
Tachikawa Corp.	To end Nov. 1987	End Nov. 1988	750	373	−377

Source: Shukan Diamond, July 23, 1988

stock exchange's listing requirements (see also Section 6.2.3). The pattern that has emerged in Japan is that several aggressive groups of arbitrageurs have, with the use of funds raised from a variety of sources, begun to seek out assets-rich companies, or those whose stock prices have remained at a relatively low level, despite their relatively high net assets value, because of "image" problems or obviously poor management. These shares are then purchased in sufficient numbers to give the arbitrageurs a significant level of control over the management of the companies, before subsequent resale at a profit.

Serious American or European potential investors may find it helpful to obtain practical assistance from such arbitrageurs. Although the Japanese public might regard such an approach as "piracy," and strong opposition might be encountered, it may still be the easiest and most effective way to acquire the controlling interest in a Japanese company.

5.6 THE ROLE OF THE JAPANESE GOVERNMENT

It is vitally important that potential American or European investors understand the role of the Japanese government. Westerners, particularly Americans, judging perhaps on the basis of their past experiences with the US Department of Justice and/or the US Federal Trade Commission, often make the mistake of assuming that the relationship between industry and government in Japan is adversarial. In the US, the federal antitrust authorities are basically very negative toward acquisitions, and procedurally very strict, as shown by the prior filing requirement under the Hart–Scott–Rodino Antitrust Improvement Act and the merger guidelines established by the Department of Justice. One question that American businessmen frequently ask is whether they are correct in believing that strict Japanese government regulations make mergers and acquisitions very difficult to carry out. It would be an understatement to say that their suspicions are entirely incorrect.

While Japan has its own antitrust legislation and the equivalent of the Federal Trade Commission, that is the Fair Trade Commission (FTC), which is responsible for enforcement, a review of Japan's postwar antitrust administration history reveals that there have been virtually no cases in which proposed mergers between large companies, or acquisitions by them, have been blocked by FTC opposition. In fact, the reverse is true. Many large-scale transactions have been carried out with considerable assistance from, and under the administrative guidance of, government agencies, particularly MITI and the Ministry of Transport (MOT), which have often succeeded in subduing FTC opposition. Such mergers and acquisitions are often referred to as "government-promoted," but do they have any significant common characteristics?

During the Meiji era, which began in 1868, the Imperial Government of Japan gave top priority to the improvement of the nation's wealth, its defense capabilities, and the boosting of industrial productivity. The government was eager to foster the growth of Japanese industry, either directly or indirectly, particularly by the setting up of *zaibatsu*, financial combines, by large Japanese businesses through merger and acquisition activity. In a sense, this policy has been inherited by Japan's post-1945 government, which played a very active role in the early postwar years in particular, promoting merger and acquisition activity in order to rebuild Japanese industry as quickly as possible and make it internationally competitive.

The Nippon Steel Corporation (NSC) is perhaps one of the best examples of this traditional policy. NSC was originally set up in 1933 as a result of a merger between Yawata Steel Mills (then owned and operated by the government), Kamaishi and Wanishi Steel Mills (then in the hands of the Mitsui Group), Kanefutaura and Kyushu Steel Mills (then owned and operated by the Mitsubishi Group), and the Fuji Steel Corporation, in order to implement the government policy of consolidating national steel production. Although in the aftermath of World War II NSC was split by the Allied Powers into several smaller companies, including the reconstituted Yawata and Fuji steel corporations, Yawata and Fuji, with strong MITI backing, amalgamated as equal partners in 1970 to form the present NSC, the largest steel manufacturer in the world today.

The list of similar merger cases promoted or sponsored by the government is almost endless. Mitsui O.S.K. Lines Ltd was formed in 1964 as a result of a merger, on a 50–50 basis, between the Osaka Steamship Co. Ltd, which was a member of the Sumitomo Bank Group, and Mitsui Lines Co. Ltd, which was part of the Mitsui Bank Group. This merger was actively promoted by the MOT in order to implement its policy of restructuring the Japanese shipping industry, which at that time consisted of 22 shipping companies, including nine oil tanker operators. The MOT sought to improve Japan's international competitiveness by reducing internal competition in the industry. This policy, unheard of in the US, is still followed today.

A similar merger took place in the banking industry in 1971, when the Nippon Kangyo Bank and the Dai-Ichi Bank were brought together on an equal footing with the assistance of the MOF; a move aimed at improving the international competitiveness of Japanese financial institutions, particularly commercial banks. In terms of the amount of deposits received, the Dai-Ichi Bank is now the largest commercial bank in the world.

As a result of a similar policy with regard to the oil industry, the Daikyo, Maruzen, and Cosmo oil companies merged in April 1986, each gaining equal rights in the new company. The acquisition of the Heiwa Sogo Bank by the Sumitomo Bank in 1986 also took place under the MOF's strong administrative guidance.

Thus it can be seen that, despite the existence of the FTC, the Japanese government as a whole has continued to back mergers and acquisitions, particularly those involving large businesses, with a view to improving the international competitiveness of Japanese industry, and with the parallel aims of rationalizing, modernizing, and reducing excessive internal competition.

Even in the case of smaller businesses, about which the government tends to be less concerned, it has become an established practice for the parties involved to visit the relevant government agencies to notify them of their merger or acquisition proposals beforehand, although there is no legal obligation to do so. In this way, the government is always kept well informed. Potential foreign investors would do well to comply with this informal practice: it would be welcomed by the government bureaucrats, and could well bring about future rewards.

While in Japan many retired high-ranking government officials are now working for industrial associations, foreign corporations doing business in Japan, or Japanese corporations owned and controlled by foreign companies and investors, are denied membership of such associations, and therefore cannot use the associations, or their representatives, for purposes of liaison or lobbying. Therefore, the easiest way for such corporations and investors to secure access to government agencies might be to hire retired high-ranking officials directly, particularly people with experience of the influential MITI, MOT, and MOF. However, very few of these companies seem prepared to accept retired Japanese government officials as members of their senior executive teams. One exception is Schlumberger Ltd, a French corporation based in New York. Schlumberger Japan has recruited a former MITI deputy minister as chairman of its board of directors, and the company has thus been able to establish friendly relations with MITI, which is responsible, amongst others, for the oil and oil-related industries. The Hilton Hotels Group also has a retired high-level MOF official among its senior executives.

This close Japanese contact with government, less usual elsewhere in the world, often proves to be very valuable, making many business operations, including mergers and acquisitions, far easier than they would otherwise be. This is especially true in regulated industries such as finance or transportation, with which the MOF and MOT are respectively concerned.

5.7 FIRST CONTACT WITH THE TARGET COMPANY: USEFUL HINTS

5.7.1 Etiquette in the initial approach

When an acquiring company has identified a suitable Japanese company as a target, the next step is to determine how to convey its intention, and what form that intention should take. This initial contact can often be crucially important in Japan, and success often depends on with whom the initial contact is made, and who acts as intermediary. The chairman or president of a Japanese company is often merely a "paper tiger," with no real power or authority, unless he also happens to be the owner of a substantial proportion of the shares. In addition, the board of directors is often split in its reaction to an acquisition offer. Before making an approach, the acquiring company must do its research carefully, and ensure that it is dealing with the pro-acquisition faction. The main bank or managing securities firm should usually have the most reliable, most up-to-date information about the target company. Sending an unsolicited letter directly to the target company's top executive, a popular practice in America and Europe, is definitely not to be recommended!

5.7.2 Shares and transfer of the ownership record

If the target company is a public company, an acquiring company usually begins to purchase shares on the open market. It is not important whether this is done before, simultaneously

121

with, or after the initial contact. Nor is there any law in Japan requiring such share transactions to be reported to the government.

However, what is important is when the transfer of ownership of the block of shares should be recorded on the books and records of the target company. If a friendly acquisition is intended, the acquiring company should make its approach with the prior approval of, or at least prior notice to, the target company's management. In Japan, if an investor were to purchase a substantial block of shares of a public company and then request transfer of ownership of those shares without at least prior notice to the company, he would probably be viewed as hostile, or as a speculative arbitrageur whose true investment purpose was to make a quick buck by forcing the company to repurchase the shares.

This being the case, when an acquiring company begins to buy shares in the target company, and before its intention to acquire has been made explicit, it must be very careful not to reveal any substantial share-dealing activities to third parties – in particular the target company itself.

It is obviously best to purchase the shares as cheaply as possible. Unfortunately, the market soon seems to become aware of what is going on – no matter how discreet the acquiring company may be – and this usually pushes the target company's share price up substantially, or makes it very volatile. One of the major reasons why this happens is that in Japan the statutory regulations prohibiting insider trading are hardly enforced at all; nor is secrecy maintained as strictly as it is in the US or Europe.

In 1988, the Securities Bureau of the MOF, the Japanese counterpart of the American SEC, amended the Securities and Exchange Act to facilitate the enforcement of the insider trading regulations, and announced its intention to take all possible preventive measures. However, the confidentiality of inside information and the prohibition of its use for stock trading purposes are not widely accepted in the Japanese business community; and the regulations remain difficult to enforce.

In fact, with reference to the completion of NSC's acquisition of Sankyo Seiki (see Section 2.4.1), it was reported in August 1988 that 34 of the two companies' employees, including four or five key personnel who were members of the acquisition project team, had purchased Sankyo Seiki shares immediately prior to the public announcement. However, the MOF and the Tokyo Stock Exchange were unable to indict them on charges of insider trading, despite the fact that the same provision as the US Rule 10b-5 exists in the Japanese Securities and Exchange Act. American and European potential investors should take careful note.

5.7.3 Initial concealment of your intentions

When the right target company, and the right board member within it, have been properly identified, it is very important to consider how the initial approach should be made. An outright "We want to acquire your company" is taboo in Japan. Words such as "acquisition" or "takeover" should be replaced with terms such as "business arrangement" or "cooperation program" (see Section 3.1), whatever the eventual intention.

The acquiring company should tell the target company that its main interest is to enter into a mutually profitable business arrangement or form of cooperation, to expand the business of both companies in Japan and to enable the target company to diversify its business in Japan and elsewhere. The target company should also be able to inspect a master plan of this proposed arrangement. It may be acceptable for the acquiring company to say that it is willing to consider making an equity participation in the target company, or perhaps a mutual equity arrangement, and it may be possible to go as far as suggesting that equity participation is desirable or even necessary to make the proposed arrangement work well. However, any word that has any connotation to do with "acquisition," "takeover," or "control" must be avoided; nor should the desirability of a majority or controlling interest be mentioned. Even a statement expressing a desire to become the largest shareholder is harmful during the early stages of negotiation.

In the first letter of proposal, emphasis should be placed on a mutually profitable business tie-up or cooperative arrangement, together with a concrete explanation of the benefits accruing to the target company from the proposed arrangement. There must be no hint whatsoever of the underlying real intention. In Japan there is an old expression that describes a foolish disguise: *Koromo no shita kara yoroi ga mieru* (literally, "To inadvertently show a part of the shining armor that is worn under a priest's robe"). The target company is likely to become extremely sensitive when it receives the first proposal, even one couched in the terms set out above, and the slightest hint of the real intention would undoubtedly put the target company on the defensive and prevent further progress. In the American and European business communities, it is commonplace to stress how the shareholders would benefit from the proposed acquisition, but it is important to stress that in Japan this type of statement is meaningless, because companies are normally considered to belong to the employees and company officers.

5.7.4 Third-party allotment and mutual equity participation

In Japan, when a company makes equity participation in another company, it often takes the form of the purchase of additional shares through "third-party allotment" (private placement) or mutual equity participation. Therefore it is advisable for American and European potential investors to employ one of these two methods when they first acquire shares. "Third-party allotment" is described in Chapter 6.

Because of its reciprocal nature, the idea of mutual equity participation fits particularly well with a package deal such as a business link-up consisting of equity arrangements on the one hand and cross-licensing, a distributorship, or the sharing of R & D facilities on the other. The arrangement between Morinaga and Fujiya, mentioned earlier, was made using mutual equity participation as leverage.

Mutual equity participation is very common in Japan, particularly between banks and their client companies, and, among nonbank corporations between, for example, manufacturers and distributors, and suppliers and purchasers. At the end of March 1987, Sanyo Electric owned more than 200 million common shares of other listed companies, with an aggregate book value of ¥54.0 billion. This included 53 million shares of the Sumitomo Bank, 28 million shares of the Kyowa Bank, 10 million Kubota shares and 6.5 million Nissan Motors shares. Because of the sharp appreciation of the market value of these shares, this holding represents a substantial part of Sanyo's huge "hidden assets."

5.7.5 Informal preliminary contact with government agencies

Under the current foreign exchange regulations, a foreign investor, whether an individual, a corporation, or whatever, is required to make a prior notification to the Japanese government through the Bank of Japan before acquiring, in any manner, 10% or more ownership of a Japanese listed company, or any shares in a nonlisted Japanese company. Direct investment from abroad has become so substantially liberalized that it is now very unlikely (as explained in Chapter 7) that the Japanese government would oppose the acquisition of a Japanese company by a foreign investor, unless the proposal affects a sensitive area of industrial policy, or touches upon national security.

Nevertheless, it is generally advisable for foreign corporate and individual investors who want to purchase a substantial block of shares in a Japanese company, or even acquire a company, to make preliminary informal contact (*nemawashi* in Japanese) with the relevant government agencies before they submit a formal notification. It is a long-established practice in Japan that informal contact, with all parties involved, precedes a formal approach whenever one tries to open a new business or make a new transaction. The main purpose of *nemawashi* is to "prime the pump" – to inform all parties involved beforehand, so as to generate a favorable opinion. In the absence of any *nemawashi*, a government agency would often express surprise, and be more nervous and cautious than it might otherwise be.

The case of *Trafalgar* vs. *Minebea* (explained fully in Section 6.1) is perhaps the best example of how things can go wrong. Trafalgar Grain tried to purchase a substantial block of Minebea's common shares in an attempt to acquire Minebea, but while a prior notification was lodged with the Japanese government through the Bank of Japan (as required by the foreign exchange regulations), the concept of *nemawashi* was ignored. Confronted with an unexpected formal notification, the government agency was probably perplexed: after all, it had no knowledge of Trafalgar, nor what its purpose was. The ensuing government caution and unnecessary bureaucratic delay were one of the major factors that prevented Trafalgar from making a successful acquisition.

5.8 THE SHAREHOLDING PERCENTAGE AND ITS IMPLICATIONS

5.8.1 The largest shareholder and his status

The largest shareholder in a Japanese corporation generally has more influence than his actual shareholding percentage would suggest. American and European readers may be surprised to learn that it is not uncommon for the largest shareholder to exercise virtual control over a company even though his holding is less than 50%. The term "largest shareholder" itself means just that: he has the largest single holding, but not necessarily a majority of the shares, nor even as much as one-third. The largest shareholder of a listed corporation often owns less than 10%.

But how can such a small holding confer virtual control over the company? It is important to deal with this thoroughly, so that potential foreign investors will understand how it is that they can gain effective control over Japanese companies without having to acquire a majority interest.

One of the answers to this question lies in the voting behavior of Japanese shareholders at shareholders' meetings. In Japan, as elsewhere, supreme corporate decision-making takes place at the shareholders' meeting, with the shareholders as the ultimate decision-makers. However, despite Japan's democratic political structure, the cult of the individual – the principle of independent thought and action – is not fully established in Japanese society. At the end of March 1988, the total number of issued and outstanding common shares of all listed Japanese corporations reached 292,968,909,942, of which 23.6% (or 69.1 billion shares, with a market value of ¥88 trillion) were owned by individual investors, and the remaining 76.4% by corporations, including institutional investors and trusts. And yet within the business community, and at meetings of the shareholders of stock corporations in particular, even corporate shareholders tend to follow a "follow the leader" behavior pattern.

This behavior stems primarily from the "bottom-up" decision-making process which is peculiar to Japanese corporations, as opposed to the "top-down" process which is commonplace in America or Europe. This "bottom-up" process tends to work as follows. When the corporation for which he works has to make a decision, the person at the lowest level in the corporate hierarchical decision-making structure puts forward an initial proposal. This in turn is submitted to a succession of direct superiors for approval, until it reaches the desk of the chief executive officer for his final approval. Unfortunately, the system is open to a certain amount of abuse. Decision-makers at the bottom or at any intermediate hierarchical level may try to make decisions which seem most acceptable or pleasing to their immediate superiors, rather than using their independent judgment to make decisions which are in the best interests of the company. In this way, they hope to avoid any detrimental consequences if anything goes wrong.

It is worth looking in detail at how a final corporate action in the form of a shareholders' resolution is actually made by this "bottom-up" process.

About four years ago, when venture business was booming in Japan, there was a certain "high-tech" venture business company, which had initially been set up by four entrepreneurs, including an engineer who was a former employee of a certain major corporation. The company, which was one of the two largest and most prominent such companies at the time, successfully implemented a fund-raising program. This became the largest single venture capital financing transaction ever made in Japan: the company raised some ¥8 billion in venture capital from a group of investors including commercial banks, securities firms, life insurance companies, and several other major corporations, with the assistance of a certain major securities firm.

Soon after the completion of this financing operation, serious differences of opinion arose among the four founders with regard to operational and managerial policies, and internal strife erupted. The founders, who were also directors and executive officers, soon divided into two equal factions, one pro-president and the other antipresident. The antipresident faction successfully voted out the incumbent president, and launched a campaign to inform the shareholders of the nature and extent of the difficulties that the company was allegedly facing, and of the alleged incompetence of the president. The pro-president faction launched a similar, counter-campaign. The dispute was finally put before the assembled shareholders, who now had to decide where they stood on the issue when exercising their voting rights.

At the meeting, the Japanese corporate shareholders adopted typical behavior: all of them, without exception, followed the so-called "blind follow suit" pattern. Without recourse to any independent analysis, they simply asked the largest shareholder how it would vote, and followed accordingly.

Their behavior was also a consequence of the "bottom-up" process, which normally operates as follows. In the case of each corporate shareholder, the person on the bottom rung of the decision-making ladder has to prepare what is known as a *ringuisho* – a presentation document describing a proposed corporate course of action, and seeking a superior's approval – in which he has to propose how his company should vote, together with his reasons. He invariably seeks a solution which, if proven wrong later, can still be justified, so that he, and those further up the ladder, cannot be personally discredited. Faced with only two possible choices, pro- or antipresident, there is only one decision that he can safely make – to recommend that his company should follow its fellow shareholders. In the firm belief that the other corporate shareholders will follow the lead given by the largest shareholder, why should his company be the exception to the rule? Believe it or not, this is indeed the most common guiding principle of Japanese businessmen.

The person on the lowest rung in the largest shareholding corporation behaves in a complementary way. According to the above principle, he expects that all of the other corporate shareholders will follow his company's example. But he cannot announce his intention publicly in advance – after all, that is counter to the guiding principle. His first course of action is to advise his superiors to cast the company's vote with the other shareholders, and then some typically Japanese groundwork or *nemawashi* follows, to establish an unspoken consensus.

129

The mention of "groundwork" here does not suggest any kind of overt or explicit action. Rather, the normal course of events is for cocktail or dinner parties to be held, separately and on a very informal basis, with a representative or representatives of each of the other corporate shareholders. Enough discreet hints are dropped to enable the representatives to understand how his company is going to vote. These informal soirées are held in hierarchical order, starting with a representative or representatives of the second largest shareholder, and then proceeding to the third, and so on, until he feels confident that an unspoken consensus has been reached. This process of "following suit" is inevitable in a situation in which nobody wants to take any responsibility for the consequences when recommending a course of action!

This pattern becomes even more noticeable when the largest shareholder is a major corporation: no one is prepared to rock the boat. It has to be said that some Japanese despise themselves for this evasive, peace-at-any-price attitude, which probably has its origins in the typical Japanese disposition of hating to create or be involved in confrontation in day-to-day life. Interestingly enough, there were two shareholders who did not follow suit in the above example: one was American and the other European.

There are two obvious lessons which can be learnt from this. First, a potential foreign investor really needs the cooperation of the largest shareholder. If he can persuade the largest shareholder to sell his holding, then he can expect the others to follow suit, and he has the *de facto* controlling interest, even if the block that he is going to purchase represents a minority of the total issued and outstanding shares. Second, if he succeeds in buying part of the largest shareholder's block of shares, he will be accorded the same degree of respect that was formerly accorded to that largest shareholder, so that he will be virtually able to participate in the largest shareholder's control over the company.

Therefore, the potential investor need not buy a majority holding, nor even 33⅓% (the threshold percentage which gives the holder thereof the effective power of veto over any proposed changes to the company's articles of incorporation). All he has to do is to purchase sufficient shares to (i) achieve "largest shareholder" status, or (ii) become a major shareholder *and* obtain the cooperation of the existing largest shareholder which, in the case of a listed company, is often a bank (see Section 5.1.3).

5.8.2 Legal rights and privileges of shareholders

Following on from the above discussion of *de facto* control, readers will of course be interested to know what statutory rights and privileges are accorded to shareholders under the terms of the Commercial Code.

From the strict legal point of view, an absolute controlling interest can only be conferred on an investor who holds at least two-thirds of the issued and outstanding voting shares. In Japan, the board of directors has, and exercises, the authority to manage the company's operations, and any person or group claiming an absolute controlling interest must have the power to appoint board members. Directors are usually elected for a term of two years. If an acquisition takes place during the board's period of office, the acquiring party can only gain absolute control by replacing the incumbent directors with its own appointees. The Commercial Code provides that a resolution to remove a director of a company can be validly passed only by a two-thirds majority vote at a meeting of its shareholders, at which shareholders holding, in aggregate, the majority of its issued and outstanding voting shares at that time are present or represented. A resolution to appoint a director can be passed by a simple majority vote.

In other words, theoretically, if a shareholder or a group of shareholders owns 66⅔% or more of the issued and outstanding voting shares of a company, the incumbent directors can immediately be removed and replaced. This 66⅔% stock ownership is also an important threshold for various other purposes, such as amending or modifying the company's articles of incorporation, approving a proposed merger, or approving a transfer of all, or substantially all, of the assets of a corporation.

In reality, however, it is quite rare for the acquiring company to have to remove the incumbent directors by force: they usually volunteer their resignations as soon as it becomes apparent that they will not be re-elected upon expiration of their current term of office. Therefore, from a practical point of view, 66⅔% ownership is not necessary for this purpose.

In order to acquire absolute control over a reasonably short period of time, rather than immediately, it is necessary to have more than 50% ownership. If an incumbent director then reaches the end of his term of office, he can be replaced by an appointee of the acquiring company on the basis of a simple majority vote at a shareholders' meeting; and the entire board can be similarly replaced over a two-year period. Few Japanese corporations, whether listed or unlisted, have in their articles of incorporation a provision allowing for cumulative voting for the election of directors, and so a simple majority is usually sufficient. Although the Commercial Code includes the provision that an ordinary resolution can be passed at a shareholders' meeting by a simple majority, assuming that shareholders holding a majority of the issued and outstanding shares are present or are represented, a party who owns more than 25% but less than an outright majority cannot always prevail. To be absolutely certain, it is best to own a majority of shares.

A 33⅓% ownership is just enough to enable a minority shareholder to exercise the power of veto against important proposed corporate plans of action (including changes to the articles of incorporation, merger approval, and assets transfers, as outlined above). Since many important aspects of company operation – including its business purposes, the location of its principal place of business, its capitalization, and the numbers of directors and statutory auditors – are provided for in the articles of incorporation, 33⅓% or more share ownership gives a minority shareholder significant influence, and the company can no longer take any important corporate action without that shareholder's consent. In this sense, 33⅓% ownership is crucial for a foreign investor who desires to acquire a Japanese company.

In an actual acquisition scenario, however, share ownership of less than 66⅔%, and even of less than 33⅓%, does not necessarily mean that little can be accomplished because, in general, not all shareholders are present or represented at most shareholders' meetings. This can be a very important factor, particularly when the acquiring company's share holding is very similar to that of the opposing shareholders.

Under the terms of the Commercial Code, a shareholder or group of shareholders holding various other percentages of the voting shares of a company is entitled to exercise a range of rights and privileges. For example, a shareholder who has, for six months or more, continuously owned at least 1% of the shares, or a number of shares that is equivalent to at least 300 Statutory Voting Units, whichever is less, is entitled to put forward propositions and to vote at shareholders' meetings. (One Statutory Voting Unit generally represents voting shares that have an aggregate par value of ¥50,000.) A 3% or more ownership for at least six months continuously entitles the holder to convene a shareholders' meeting; while a holding of at least 10% entitles the investor to inspect, and to copy or make excerpts from, the company's accounts ledgers and other records. These rights and privileges can, of course, be used to put psychological pressure on company management.

In an acquisition scenario, these minor rights and privileges amount to very little, and 33⅓% remains an essential threshold. However, any shareholder, no matter how small his holding, is entitled to inspect the register of shareholders of the company. This right of inspection is particularly important for a shareholder hoping to acquire the company by tender offer, because sooner or later he must find out who the other shareholders are and how much they own. If his request to inspect, copy, or make excerpts from the register is refused, he can obtain a court order to force the company to disclose the information.

In most friendly acquisition cases in Japan, the acquiring party is given *de facto* control over the target company as a result of a "gentlemen's agreement" reached after negotiations between the two management teams, without having to acquire a controlling interest.

In Japan, most acquiring companies tend to tread gently. They are unlikely to be too forthright about acquiring the absolute controlling interest, for fear of humiliating, frightening, discouraging, or demoralizing both management and employees. Similarly, they are unlikely to be in a hurry to replace all of the senior management personnel of the target company with their appointees. The president is likely to be replaced, but other senior personnel retained, while one or two additional senior management staff (often retired main bank officials) may be seconded as board members or special advisers to show the acquiring company's generosity and willingness to support the target company's independence. Needless to say, all this is done to avoid any impression of "raiding," and at the same time to give the employees the feeling of "continued" independence in order to keep morale in good shape. Most Japanese company owners and senior executives believe that the success of an acquisition should be judged by the subsequent performance of the target company, rather than the acquisition, or otherwise, of an outright controlling interest. Accordingly, they will make the utmost efforts to prevent demoralization and to minimize opposition.

5.9 TIMING: PUBLIC DISCLOSURES AND PRESS RELEASES

One of the essential keys to successful acquisitions in Japan is the maintenance of secrecy. Particularly in the case of friendly acquisitions, it is vital to prevent the press and other news media from finding out that negotiations are under way. In the case of acquisitions of or by listed corporations, even greater care is needed, because premature disclosures might lead to undue fluctuations in the market price of the target corporation's stock – and the price can fluctuate to such an extent that the acquisition attempt may be spoiled completely.

In Japan, listed companies are obliged to make timely disclosures of their corporate affairs to protect the interests of their investors, just as their American or European counterparts do. From time to time the Tokyo Stock Exchange (TSE) sends circulars to companies whose securities are listed or traded on the exchange, requiring them to make timely disclosures, in an attempt to reduce the chances of insider trading. In these notices, the TSE requests that the timely disclosure of all available data and information regarding corporate affairs that may have some bearing on the investment decisions of investors should be made to the general public through the nationwide news media. Nevertheless, the determination of what should be disclosed, how that information is related to any proposed transactions, and whether or not such transactions are realistic is left up to each individual listed corporation. Corporations are expected to use their own best judgment, with regard to both the nature and extent of the disclosure.

Despite this TSE requirement, secrecy is often given top priority during acquisition negotiations in Japan. In most cases, a public announcement is made just before a transaction is completed or, if the acquisition is subject to material uncertainties, immediately following the full execution and delivery of the acquisition agreement. Thus in a normal Japanese case, the "timely disclosure" can occur much later than it would have to in the US. For example, the press release announcing Nippon Steel's acquisition of Sankyo Seiki (see Section 2.4.1) was published on July 29, 1988, a month after the signature of the stock purchase agreement on June 30.

It is very difficult to maintain secrecy in Japan. It is not rare for proposed acquisitions to become the subject of press "scoops," as a result of a reporter having his ear very close to the ground, or due to a premature and unintentional leak by an insider. Ironically, in this way the public receives its "timely disclosure" early – and very much in line with American standards!

5.10 NOTICES TO STOCK EXCHANGES

Each individual corporation whose shares or securities are listed on the Tokyo Stock Exchange is required by the regulations of the exchange promptly to notify it of any event or circumstance which is likely to affect its affairs, financial status, or performance. The regulations also require such corporations to give prior notice to the exchange if they have reason to believe that any such circumstance is likely to arise. Individual corporations are expected to exercise their own discretion in determining whether or not the possible circumstance is worth reporting, and whether or not the predicted outcome is assessed accurately and reasonably. In actual practice, most corporations are so discreet about this sort of thing that the required notice is not made until the very last moment. In particular, when a listed corporation is acquired by a nonlisted company, the required notice to the exchange is often not made at the time of the execution of the acquisition agreement but just before the final closing of the deal, because the parties involved usually do not want to attract any unnecessary attention or close scrutiny, lest the exchange should step in to prevent what is known as a "backdoor listing."

5.10.1 Backdoor listing

The term "backdoor listing," as used in connection with the acquisition by a nonlisted company of a listed company, refers to the way in which a nonlisted company merges with a listed company after acquisition so that it can adopt the name of the listed company as its company or group name. In so doing, an unlisted company can acquire listed status, effectively circumventing the stringent listing standards of the stock exchange. Stock exchanges in Japan, including Tokyo, have taken a hardline approach to attempted backdoor listings. In Japan, unlike America or Europe, it can be a great asset to have listed status: it ensures improved creditworthiness, which in turn guarantees greater ease in raising funds from capital or credit markets. Listed status is regarded as a privilege, and the stock exchanges consider it their duty to protect it by preventing backdoor listings.

To avoid being criticized in this way, a nonlisted company which has successfully acquired a listed company usually refrains from a number of activities – merging, changing the listed company's name, transferring all or substantially all of its business and assets to the listed company, or acquiring seats on the listed company's board – at least for some time after completion of the acquisition. As soon as an acquisition of this kind is completed, a serious tug-of-war begins backstage, between the relevant stock exchange and the nonlisted company. The stock exchange does its best to prevent the privilege of the acquired listed company from being transferred to the nonlisted company, while the latter does all that it can to benefit from that privilege.

5.11 LABOR RELATIONS

When acquiring a Japanese company, two problems to do with labor relations have to be taken into consideration: the first is how to deal with the labor unions before the deal is finalized, and the second is how to deal with them after the deal has gone through.

The following example may suggest factors that are important if a deal is to be successfully completed. Several years ago, an American company tried to sell one of its wholly owned Japanese subsidiaries as part of a restructuring plan. Although it contacted several potential Japanese purchasers, the deal failed to materialize because of labor problems. While the negotiations for sale were under way, the Japanese subsidiary became involved in a tough legal battle with two of its former employees who had been dismissed. Both alleged that their dismissal had been unlawful, and that they should be reinstated. In Japan, it can take years to resolve a legal action of this kind, which often embitters relations between labor and management. Naturally, all of the potential purchasers invariably insisted that the proposed deal could only go through on condition that the pending law suits be finally settled, either in or out of court, at the seller's expense. Realizing that it had no choice but to settle with the plaintiffs in order to close the case, the seller began to make vigorous but futile efforts to negotiate with the plaintiffs' communist labor union. All offers were rejected by the plaintiffs and their union, who argued that they were not concerned about financial compensation. Eventually, the discouraged potential purchasers pulled out.

However, the truth of the matter is that money was indeed the prime concern: the unions covertly demanded substantial settlement payments, payments that were simply too large for the plaintiffs' former employer or the parent company to accept. Theoretically, if the Japanese subsidiary had agreed to pay any amount in settlement, its net assets value would have been correspondingly reduced, and a potential purchaser would have been entitled to a reduction in the purchase price. However, the American parent company tried to persuade the potential purchasers to share the cost of the settlement payments, and the potential purchasers found this to be totally unacceptable.

While the fact that employees are represented by a labor union or unions does not by itself pose an insurmountable problem, the existence of any serious labor disputes between the target company and any of the labor unions certainly does. When a labor union, or members involved in a labor dispute, become aware that a third party is attempting to acquire the company, settlement demands tend to become extravagant. This naturally discourages the third party, not only because of the financial impact on the target company, but also because of the serious problem of whether or not the target company, even if acquired, would remain liable for the outcome of the dispute.

American and European potential investors have little experience of dealing with labor disputes in Japan, which often involve tough communist unions. The best policy is to avoid involvement altogether, by trying to eliminate, from lists of potential acquisitions, any target companies which have serious labor disputes pending. Even in the absence of serious disputes, a Japanese labor union may still oppose an attempted acquisition because it fears that its employees will become subject to American and European labor practices such as layoffs or redundancies.

In theory, the opinion of the labor unions can be disregarded, because they are not parties to the acquisition transaction; but in practice target company managements are often hesitant to sign acquisition agreements if the labor unions representing their employees oppose the action. The ability to persuade and appease labor unions is one of the keys to success. Even in wholly Japanese acquisitions, it is not uncommon for the investor to obtain the prior consent of the labor unions involved.

As demonstrated in each of the Misawa Homes acquisition cases, Mr Misawa himself spent several days meeting the employees of the target company, in order to hear their comments and of course to sway them to his point of view. Similarly, Mr Ushioda, the chief executive of the Toyo Sash Group, is also said to have made it his policy to visit each of the factories of the company that his group was about to acquire, to talk directly to employees. He is reported to have repeatedly stressed that past poor performance should be blamed on senior management, not the workforce themselves, and to stress that their future security would be assured.

One of the difficulties encountered by American and European companies which seek to make acquisitions in Japan is that their senior executives are simply not in a position to take a similar course of action. They can of course talk to Japanese employees and labor unions through an interpreter, but it is very difficult – if not impossible – to convey exactly what they want to say; and the Japanese workforce are likely to be put on the defensive if they have to come face to face with high-powered foreign business executives. One practical way to overcome this problem is to retain as many of the Japanese board members as possible, at least for a while, and let them talk to the employees. If, for some reason, it is necessary to remove the existing board members from office quickly, then at least the office of president should be filled by a Japanese national, who can then talk to and persuade the employees on behalf of his principal.

A carefully thought out strategy such as this, even before an acquisition has been completed, will lay the foundations for the establishment of continuing friendly relations.

Nowadays, with thousands of foreign or foreign-capital-based firms operating in Japan, the Japanese, particularly those living in urban areas, have become quite accustomed to working for, or under the direction of, people of very different ethnic backgrounds. Nevertheless, linguistic and cultural barriers remain, and successful post-acquisition labor management can depend to a considerable extent on whether or not the new owner retains qualified Japanese personnel in key positions after the acquisition.

The Minebea company, one of the most highly acquisition-oriented companies in Japan, provides a good example. Minebea's principal owner, Mr Takami Takahashi, is a labor relations specialist and was once executive vice-chairman of the labor union of the Kanebo Corporation, one of Japan's leading synthetic textile and chemical manufacturers. With Minebea's attempted hostile acquisition of Sankyo Seiki – perhaps the first such attempt by a listed company in Japan to acquire another listed company – in stalemate for over two years, Mr Takahashi approached the Sankyo Seiki employees directly to try to break the deadlock (despite the fact that Minebea owned less than 20% of Sankyo Seiki at the time). By direct mail, he told Sankyo Seiki employees that the proposed merger between the two companies would do them no harm, in the belief that his best chance of success was to drive a wedge between Sankyo Seiki's employees and its current management. To counter this, the Sankyo Seiki management bought newspaper advertising space to tell Minebea that while it was free to purchase shares on the open market in the normal way, it was totally unfair to approach the employees directly in an obvious attempt to unsettle their confidence and trust in their current management.

In reply to this, Mr Takahashi publicly argued that he still believed the merger to be in the best interests of both companies: that Sankyo Seiki had been so slow to internationalize its operations that it would not be able to cope with the current "high yen" economy unless the merger took place (Minebea being allegedly fully internationalized); and that the proposed merger was the best way for Sankyo Seiki to survive on a viable basis and protect the jobs of its employees. Thus both sides tried very hard to obtain the recognition and support of Sankyo Seiki's employees and their labor union.

There is no set rule stipulating exactly when the management of a target company should tell its labor unions that negotiations are in progress, and try to obtain the unions' support. Each case should be handled according to the prevalent circumstances. If the labor union is a cooperative intra-company union (which is usually the case in Japan – see Section 6.2.13 for related issues) with no record of serious labor disputes, the best time would be immediately before or just after the execution of the acquisition agreement. On the other hand, if the target company has had to deal with a radical labor union, or there have been serious disputes, it is advisable to notify the union either at a much earlier or much later stage.

5.12 AUDIT AND INVESTIGATION OF THE TARGET COMPANY

5.12.1 An acquisition audit by a CPA

There is no significant difference between America or Europe and Japan when it comes to the methodology and timing of the essential audit of a target company. First-hand information must be diligently obtained about the company's legal and credit standing, and its financial position. However, American and European potential investors often encounter some common problems which, to a certain extent, are peculiar to Japan, and which will be discussed in detail in this section.

In Japan there are very few certified public accountants (CPAs) who are experienced in providing auditing services in connection with acquisitions: they are more used to rendering services required by the Securities and Exchange Act or the Commercial Code, services which are essentially similar to those rendered by American CPAs to their client corporations when preparing annual reports. Annual reports follow a set pattern, and the work is of a routine nature, but acquisition audits require considerably more, including the evaluation of intangible assets, not shown on the balance sheet, such as industrial know-how and goodwill, and the identification and location of hidden assets or liabilities. To perform such audits properly it is necessary to retain the services of the few local Japanese CPAs who have experience of this kind of work: it would be wishful thinking to rely upon one of the "Big Eight" American firms.

5.12.2 Window dressing

Window dressing is not rare in Japan: there have been a significant number of cases, involving both nonlisted and listed companies. A typical example involving a listed company is that of the Tokyo-based Riccar Corporation, already mentioned in Section 2.1.

Riccar, which was listed on the First Section of the Tokyo Stock Exchange, was almost bankrupt in 1984 and subsequently filed a petition for corporate reorganization. While the petition was pending, Riccar's receiver unearthed a staggering amount of window dressing in the company's past financial statements: as a consequence of this felony, several members of the company's previous management, including its former president, have now been criminally convicted. It does seem astonishing that this can have happened on the prestigious First Section at Tokyo.

All listed companies in Japan are subject to periodical audit by CPAs, just as in the US and Europe, but this case proves that it is not impossible for the CPAs to be deceived by wilful window-dressing schemes.

It is also common knowledge in Japan that some smaller nonlisted companies are in the habit of preparing more than one set of accounts; one to show to their banks, another for the tax offices, another for their suppliers, etc. Therefore potential foreign investors should be warned that they must not jump to the conclusion that, since Japan is a fully industrialized nation, the same standards of conduct prevail as in America or Europe. Complacency may lead to severe consequences.

5.12.3 Promissory notes and hidden liabilities

A third problem is that of hidden or off-the-record debts and liabilities, including contingent liabilities. In the US and Europe, one of the most important tasks for CPAs and lawyers who are auditing and reviewing target company accounts, financial statements, books, and records is to perform what is known as the "due diligence review," to determine if and to what extent hidden liabilities exist. The same is true in Japan, except in one respect. While contingent liabilities arising from product liability or environmental actions and taxation are considered to be the two most important aspects in the US and Europe, the Japanese pay little attention to them. Product liability actions are still uncommon in Japan, and rarely result in the award of such huge amounts of damages as is often the case in the US. Similarly, pollution actions in this country rarely involve enormous amounts of damages, although there have been a few exceptions. Again, "due diligence" is required.

In Japan, all major corporations are subject to tax audits by the taxation authorities once every three years or so. This means that it is entirely possible that, after the completion of an acquisition deal, a target company may receive a visit from a team of tax investigators, who may invalidate certain tax accounting practices or options adopted by the company during the period leading up to the acquisition – and this may result in substantial tax liabilities.

An even more serious problem in Japan is the risk of exposure to hidden or contingent liabilities resulting from day-to-day transactions, which can become immense. Unlike America or Europe, most day-to-day commercial transactions in Japan are settled by promissory notes, rather than by cash or check. Promissory notes change hands by endorsement (usually with recourse) before they reach maturity, which usually ranges from three to six months. In most cases a company which has issued a promissory note will honor it and pay up at maturity, just as the recipient, endorser, or holder expects. However, this is not always the case. While every company is expected to keep detailed accounts, showing when it issued or endorsed promissory notes, and to whom, and to record the amount and date of maturity, the system does sometimes break down. A note may be issued, with or without authority, and no corresponding entry made in the accounts. Once a promissory note has been issued by or on behalf of any person or organization, it must be honored upon maturity: otherwise, the issuer will immediately incur severe penalties, such as the suspension of its bank or clearing house accounts. The really alarming aspect of Japanese abuse of promissory notes is that it is not unusual for companies in financial difficulty to issue accommodation notes, notes not issued in payment for legitimate commercial trade, but in a desperate attempt to obtain finance. Sometimes promissory notes are actually issued with the amount left completely blank, and Japanese law deems that the holder is then entitled to fill in whatever amount he likes! As you can imagine, the contingent liabilities can be enormous and, again, potential American and European investors have been warned.

6

Why American Methods
do not Apply

In this chapter, an attempt will be made to explain why typical American acquisition methods, particularly hostile acquisition through tender offers or proxy battles, are disliked in Japan, and why they often result in a very unsatisfactory and frustrating outcome.

6.1 LESSONS FROM *TRAFALGAR* VS. *MINEBEA*

In the summer of 1986, two foreign investment companies failed in their efforts to take over a large Japanese company: Trafalgar Holdings Ltd and Glen International PLC made a determined attempt to acquire Minebea, a high-tech concern. The case provides some valuable lessons for foreign investors who may be contemplating hostile mergers and acquisitions in Japan.

In early 1985, Glen International, based in the UK, was able to acquire a holding of Minebea's convertible bonds and warrant bonds. Glen subsequently purchased about 10.5 million Minebea shares on the stock exchange, so that after full conversion of the convertibles and warrants it could control about 30% of Minebea's shares.

In August 1985, the US finance company, Trafalgar Holdings, announced that it had acquired an option from Glen to purchase its current stake in Minebea. Meanwhile, Minebea began to make headlines of its own by proposing to merge with Sankyo Seiki. Trafalgar reacted by announcing its intention to acquire either Minebea or Sankyo Seiki, or both.

Minebea quickly took defensive measures. In September 1985, it issued convertible bonds worth about ¥16 billion for private placement which, if converted, would represent about 8.3% of the issued shares. The result would be to dilute Trafalgar's potential holding from 30% to only 27.7%. As an additional form of defense, Minebea also signed a merger contract with Kanemori Co. Ltd, a kimono and textile manufacturer that was already a member of the Minebea Group (see Section 6.2.7).

In February 1986, Trafalgar filed a suit in Japan, in protest at the dilution of its shareholdings, and also applied for a provisional order to block the impending merger between Minebea and Kanemori. Two days later, Trafalgar filed papers with the Japanese government seeking permission to increase its holding in Minebea to more than 10%, in effect asking to be allowed to convert its bonds and warrants into equity. However, on March 13, 1986 the MOF concluded that as some 10% of Minebea's products, such as revolvers for the Self-Defense Forces, industrial fasteners, and aircraft bolts, were defense-related, it would postpone making the decision for three months because the case involved "national security" (see also Section 5.7.5). Then, at the end of March, a Japanese District Court dismissed Trafalgar's application to block the Minebea–Kanemori merger.

In the meantime, private negotiations resulted in Nomura Securities Ltd and Daiwa Securities Ltd taking over the resale of the shares and bonds held by Trafalgar: the foreign investors had given up.

Minebea had used what tends to be the most common form of defense in Japan when a company is under threat: namely, to place large blocks of shares in the hands of stable shareholders, such as financial institutions or banks. Minebea's placement of bonds, although a novelty in Japan, had the same effect. Minebea also managed to dilute Trafalgar's holding by issuing new convertible bonds.

The merger with Kanemori was deliberately self-damaging, and intended to make Minebea a less attractive proposition: Kanemori's product lines could not be considered to complement Minebea's high-tech output and, additionally, Kanemori's sales were sluggish.

The Japanese government's reaction is noteworthy. The relevant statute allows the government the discretion to prohibit the purchase of a domestic company by a foreign investor if "the national security, public order or welfare, or . . . the national economy" could be harmed in consequence. The decision-making process, normally completed within 30 days, was stretched out to four months. During that time, Trafalgar abandoned its efforts and settled amicably, selling its holding for what it said were "substantial profits."

The informal and invisible influence of government agencies, the so-called administrative guidance, is an important factor to be considered when making takeover bids. Another factor is that Japanese companies prefer to place their shares in the care of stable shareholders. It is also important to remember that the target company's employees and shareholders have to be convinced of the merger's mutual benefits, and that the good image of the target company must not be damaged as a result of the acquisition.

Foreign investors can learn many lessons from Trafalgar's failure. First, the attempt turned out to be so typically American in style that its only achievement was to trigger rejection symptoms throughout Japanese business, financial, and governmental circles. Second, since no assiduous attempt was made to explain the mutual benefits to Minebea's shareholders, and especially to its main bank shareholders, the main bank antagonized by rather than cooperated with Trafalgar. Third, since Trafalgar did not obtain a favorable consensus of opinion amongst representatives of the Japanese government, and the leading Liberal Democratic Party, through prior informal contact, it was thoroughly snubbed and rebuked.

6.2 AVAILABLE METHODS

This section deals primarily with the available methods of acquiring Japanese companies, and simultaneously attempts to explain why American methods, particularly hostile acquisitions, are disliked and therefore have little chance of success in Japan. In general, the available methods can be classified into two categories: (A) those involving the purchase of stock; and (B) those not involving the purchase of stock.

Category A can be subdivided into:

(a) acquisitions the success of which requires no particular cooperation on the part of the target company's management; and

(b) acquisitions undertaken with their assistance and cooperation, and/or that of the shareholders.

Subcategory (a) can be further broken down into:

(i) acquisitions through the purchase of stock on the open market;

(ii) acquisitions through the purchase of convertible and/or warrant bonds issued overseas;

(iii) acquisitions through the purchase of stock from arbitrageurs;

(iv) acquisitions through the purchase of stock from a major shareholder or major shareholders, on a negotiated exchange transaction basis; and finally

(v) acquisitions through hostile tender offers.

Subcategory (b) can be further broken down into acquisitions through the purchase of (i) new stock or (ii) convertible bonds directly from the target company by means of private placement, and (iii) acquisitions through friendly tender offers.

Category B can also be subdivided into:

(a) acquisitions the success of which requires no particular cooperation on the part of the target company's management; and
(b) acquisitions undertaken with their assistance and cooperation, and/or that of the shareholders.

In this case, subcategory (a) can be broken down into:

(i)   acquisitions through merger, or through the purchase of all, or substantially all, of the target company's business assets;
(ii) replacement of the target company's management;
(iii) acquisitions through purchase of additional shares and/ or convertible bonds by means of private placement;

all of which require the solicitation of proxies. Subcategory (b) can be broken down into (i) acquisitions through merger, and acquisitions through the purchase of all, or substantially all, of (ii) the target company's business or (iii) the target company's assets.

Thus an investor has a choice of at least 14 methods, which can be used in various combinations. They are discussed in more detail below.

6.2.1   The purchase of stock on the open market

This is undoubtedly the quickest and most cost-effective way to acquire a listed or publicly held Japanese company, but it must be done covertly. As mentioned earlier, as statutory provisions prohibiting insider trading are not strictly enforced, and the maintenance of secrecy can be difficult, it is quite difficult

Table 6.1 List of companies whose percentage of nonfloating shareholders is low: the 25 lowest-ranking companies

Rank	Company	Ratio (%)
1	Heiwa Real Estate Co. Ltd	7.13
2	Nankai Electric Railway Co. Ltd	15.58
3	Teikoku Oil Co. Ltd	15.68
4	Mitsui Mining and Smelting Co. Ltd	17.85
5	Hankyu Corporation	18.08
6	Kirin Brewery Co. Ltd	18.97
7	Seika Sangyo Co. Ltd	19.48
8	Fujiko Co. Ltd	19.53
9	Kitakawa Iron Works Co. Ltd	19.62
10	Toyo Terminal Mfg. Co. Ltd	19.75
11	Noda Industrial Co. Ltd	19.86
12	Nissan Chemical Industries Ltd	20.06
13	Nippon Steel Corporation	20.10
14	Nikkatsu Corporation	21.01
15	Kawasaki Steel Corporation	21.04
16	Sony Corporation	21.42
17	Miyairi Valve Mfg. Co. Ltd	21.51
18	Unichika Ltd	21.59
19	Shinki Bus	21.60
20	Nippon Dream Kanko Co. Ltd	21.78
21	Ebara Corporation	21.80
22	Yamato Transport Co. Ltd	22.03
23	Nippon Oil Co. Ltd	22.40
24	Otori Senni Kogyo	22.48
25	Hitachi Ltd	22.62

Source: Nikkei Sangyo Shimbun, September 5, 1985

to purchase a substantial number of common shares without attracting the attention of the public. And public awareness is likely to drive the market price of the company's stock through the roof, making acquisition very costly, or simply not feasible.

It is possible, but rather difficult, to purchase shares without attracting public attention by using one or more of the major brokerage houses: difficult because the "order slips" used by brokerage houses to record transactions tend to pass through many pairs of hands. By far the best way to maintain secrecy is to use the services of professional "stock collectors," people who have the expertise and skill to purchase, on behalf of their principals, substantial numbers of stocks without attracting public attention or arousing the concern of target company managements. To do this, they usually use ten or more smaller

Table 6.2 Stockholding ratios of financial institutions: the 25 lowest-ranking companies

Rank	Company	Ratio (%)
1	Toei Chemical Industry	0.00
2	Otori Seni Kogyo	0.15
3	Kinki Eiga Genkijyo	0.21
4	Honshu Chemical Industry Co. Ltd	0.22
5	Shin Nippon Boseki	0.33
6	Zentsu Ryoko Concrete Industry	0.36
7	Gajyoen Kanko Co. Ltd	0.59
8	PS Concrete	0.59
9	Fuji Seito Co. Ltd	0.72
10	Nikkatsu Corporation	0.74
11	Wakayama Machine Tools Ltd	0.77
12	Kyoto Hotel	0.78
13	Fuji Titanium Industry	0.83
14	Daito Seiki Co. Ltd	1.17
15	Kyosan Electric Wire & Cable Co. Ltd	1.20
16	Tokyo Toyota Motor Corporation	1.29
17	Suntory Bar	1.33
18	Shimura Kako Co. Ltd	1.40
19	Terada Cotton Spinning Co. Ltd	1.41
20	Noda Industrial Co. Ltd	1.44
21	Hitachi Zosen Tomioka Machinery	1.46
22	Sanko Paper Mfg. Co. Ltd	1.47
23	Naka Nippon Kogyo	1.48
24	Nihonbashi Soko	1.50
25	Izu–Hakone Railway Co. Ltd	1.56

Source: Nikkei Sangyo Shimbun, September 5, 1985

brokerage houses. A major disadvantage of using collectors' services is that it can take from six months to as much as 18 months to acquire a substantial percentage of a target company's shares.

Table 6.1 shows details of the 25 listed companies who have the lowest percentages of their shares held by "stable sharehol-ders." In this case, the term "stable shareholder" means their respective top ten shareholders, usually banks or other financial institutions, and includes those of their respective shareholders who are company officers or board members. Similarly, in Table 6.2 are shown details of the 25 listed companies who have the lowest percentages of their shares held by banks or other financial institutions.

The lowest-ranking companies in Table 6.1 obviously have higher percentages of unstable shareholders, and are therefore easier to acquire. Table 6.2 is also very interesting, in that it clearly indicates the equity relations between the specific companies and their major banks. Again, the lowest-ranking companies obviously have weaker ties with banks, and are therefore relatively more vulnerable to acquisition attempts. Surprisingly few of the companies shown in Table 6.1 have adopted any contingency plans to discourage uninvited acquisition attempts. Kirin Brewery, which ranks sixth from the bottom, is a prime example. "We are not particularly concerned about un-invited acquisition attempts by others," says one of its senior executives, "because a huge amount of money would be re-quired to acquire our company." One of the top executives of Hitachi, which ranks 25th, has said that "We have adopted no particular scheme worth mentioning to prevent uninvited or hostile acquisition attempts." The same is true of Nippon Steel, which ranks 13th: one of its senior executive officers has been quoted as saying "We have no particular plan to increase the number of stable shareholders."

On the other hand, there are quite a few listed companies that have a substantial percentage of their shares held by stable

Table 6.3 Nonfloating share ratio: the ten highest-ranking companies

Rank	Company	Ratio (%)
1	Sanko Paper Mfg. Co. Ltd	86.86
2	Ohtsu Tire Co. Ltd	86.61
3	Toyo Bosuifu Mfg. Co. Ltd	85.28
4	Shin Nippon Drop Foreign Co. Ltd	81.40
5	Tokyo Toyota Motor Corporation	81.05
6	Zenisu Ryoko Concrete Co. Ltd	80.68
7	Fuji Steamship Co. Ltd	79.86
8	Hosui	79.82
9	PS Concrete Co. Ltd	79.73
10	Yuraku Tochi Co. Ltd	79.71

Source: Nikkei Sangyo Shimbun, September 5, 1985

Table 6.4 Stockholding ratios of financial institutions: the ten highest-ranking companies

Rank	Company	Ratio (%)
1	Nippon Housing Loan Co. Ltd	85.70
2	Kurimoto Ltd	74.39
3	Hochiki Corporation	72.96
4	Okuma Machinery Works Ltd	66.72
5	Kubota Engineering	66.56
6	Tanabe Seiyaku Co. Ltd	66.05
7	Dainippon Seiyaku	66.01
8	Noritake Co. Ltd	64.67
9	Saibu Gas Co. Ltd	64.03
10	Minolta Corporation	63.74

Source: Nikkei Sangyo Shimbun, September 5, 1985

shareholders, in the form of banks and other financial institutions. Tables 6.3 and 6.4 show the top ten companies in these categories. The Minolta Corporation, for example, has an established policy of having its banks own as many Minolta shares as possible, in order to strengthen the relationships between them. And Kubota Engineering has spent many years increasing both the number of stable shareholders and their holdings.

6.2.2 The purchase of convertible and/or warrant bonds

A number of listed Japanese companies have issued convertible and/or warrant bonds in overseas capital markets, particularly within Europe. Unlike the purchase of common shares on the stock exchange in Japan, the purchase of such bonds confers certain advantages. First, since the bonds are usually issued by private placement and are therefore owned by a limited number of institutional investors, mostly European merchant and commercial banks, they can be purchased through secret negotiation. Second, the purchase of a significant holding of such bonds does not necessarily have any immediate impact on the market price of the issuer's common stock.

There have been a number of cases in the past in which foreign investors have purchased a substantial number of these bonds in an attempt to acquire the issuing company. For example, although it did not go as far as to acquire Tokyo Sanyo Electric, one of Sanyo Electric's predecessors, a certain British investment company purchased a substantial number of Sanyo's convertible bonds in Europe a few years ago, presumably in an attempt to make an acquisition. Another example is provided by the *Trafalgar* vs. *Minebea* case, in which Trafalgar Holdings obtained the option to purchase a substantial number of Minebea's convertible bonds to use as leverage when making a tender offer.

A further example, already mentioned in Section 2.4.1, is Minebea's attempt to acquire and merge with Sankyo Seiki. Minebea, which is said to have owned less than 20% of Sankyo Seiki's issued and outstanding common shares, is said to have purchased a substantial number of the company's convertible bonds in the European capital market before it became Sankyo Seiki's largest shareholder. Since convertible bonds issued in the European capital market are issued in bearer form, and usually traded over the counter, it is virtually impossible to know who has purchased what, and for how much. As much as five million of the 14 million or so Sankyo Seiki shares owned by Minebea were acquired through the conversion of bonds, and it is said that Sankyo Seiki was totally unaware of how much of its stock had been acquired until the very last moment. It is also said that the Videosellers Group acquired much of its Fujita Tourist holding abroad, in the form of convertible bonds (see Section 5.5).

Table 6.5 shows the Japanese listed companies that have the highest ratio between the aggregate face value of their outstanding convertible bonds and their share capital. In the table, the term "PCSE ratio" means the "potential common stock equivalent ratio," the numerator of which is the number of shares issuable upon conversion of all of the company's outstanding convertible bonds, while the denominator is the total number of issued and outstanding shares, including those issuable upon conversion. Osaka Oxygen achieved its prominent position in this list by issuing a substantial number of convertible bonds to the parent company of its largest shareholder, the UK's British Oxygen, by private placement. Minebea had the second highest PCSE ratio at the time. All of the companies with high PCSE ratios naively admit that when they issued convertible bonds it had never occurred to them that the bonds might be purchased by others with a view to acquisition!

Table 6.5 Companies having a potentially large number of shares due to the issuance of foreign convertible bonds

Company	PCSE ratio (%)[a]	Number of potential shares (thousands)	Nonconverted, unexercised amount (million yen)
Osaka Oxygen Kogyo	48.04	40,331	11,220
Minebea Co. Ltd	42.93	93,821	65,718
Chujitsuya Co. Ltd	39.38	22,935	15,521
Kenwood Corporation	34.73	18,256	13,431
Gun San	33.86	11,698	4,288
Renown Inc.	23.96	37,565	27,568
Daishinpan Co. Ltd	22.85	8,845	6,609
Daido Sanso K. K.	22.48	10,070	2,537
Nakayama Steel Works Ltd	21.91	17,183	7,744
Asics Corporation	21.32	28,058	12,438
Nippon Shinpan Co. Ltd	21.15	52,930	33,619
Ryobi Ltd	20.51	24,974	10,123
Sanyo Electric Co. Ltd	20.25	6,922	8,908
Maruzen Co. Ltd	20.15	15,295	7,075
Durban Inc.	19.58	9,493	4,908
Gun Ei Chemical	19.40	10,494	9,668
Asahi Ka Forging	19.12	6,999	2,421
Tsubakimoto Precision Product Co. Ltd	18.76	6,642	9,922
Takasago Thermal Engineering Co. Ltd	18.58	8,551	4,899
Fuji Tech	18.50	11,948	8,942
Zeto	18.10	3,638	2,263
Tokyu Department Store Co. Ltd	17.96	28,862	13,889
Showa Line Ltd	17.72	27,763	5,691
Pasco Corporation	17.46	6,350	8,934
Daiichi Katei Denki Co. Ltd	17.26	11,879	7,828
Toshiba Plant	17.21	8,259	6,557
Osumi Howa	17.05	7,133	3,859
Han Wa Ko	16.93	29,101	20,567
Sonoike Tool Mfg. Co. Ltd	16.59	9,771	10,668
Sankyo Seiki Mfg. Co. Ltd	16.56	11,649	15,111
Kayaba Industry Co. Ltd	16.55	23,770	7,241
Tokyu Store Co. Ltd	16.51	6,219	5,458
Silver Seiko Ltd	16.49	7,999	4,615
Yamamura Glass Co. Ltd	16.37	12,209	6,242
Iseki & Co. Ltd	16.06	26,049	10,075

Note:
[a] The PCSE ratio is calculated on the basis of the proportion of potential shares (in the form of nonconverted debentures and unexercised warrants due to the issue of foreign bonds) to the total number of issued and outstanding shares, as of the end of July 1985.
Source: Nihon Keizai Shimbun, September 21, 1985

6.2.3 The purchase of stock from arbitrageurs

The activities of arbitrageurs in Japan have already been mentioned in Section 5.5: in this subsection their activities will be explained in further detail. In Table 6.6 are shown those listed companies whose common shares were acquired by arbitrageurs to a substantial extent in 1985, while in Table 6.7 the percentage holdings by arbitrageurs as of 1988 are listed.

Although most of the companies in the 1985 listing eventually escaped the clutches of the arbitrageurs, either by buying their shares back, or because the arbitrageur subsequently suffered financial collapse, a few are still battling it out. In 1985 there were 30 or so listed companies whose shares had been acquired by arbitrageurs to an extent of around 10%.

6.2.4 The purchase of stock directly from major shareholders

Here we consider acquisitions through the purchase of stock from major shareholders on the basis of negotiated off-exchange transactions. As mentioned in Section 5.8.1, in Japan the largest shareholder exercises considerable influence, and acquisition of all, or a substantial part of, his stake gives a new investor virtual control over a listed Japanese company. In fact, there are many Japanese listed companies which have successfully gained control over other listed companies, or large nonlisted companies, in this way: Toyo Sash, Asahi Glass, Furukawa Co. Ltd, and Misawa Homes are good examples.

Toyo Sash acquired its holding in Nittetsu Curtain Walls directly from the then largest shareholders, namely Japan Steel and Mitsui & Co. When Asahi Glass acquired Nippon Carbide in July 1984, it purchased shares directly from the latter's largest shareholders, the Mitsubishi Bank and Mitsubishi Chemical Industries. Asahi also acquired control of Elna by purchasing

Table 6.6 Listed companies whose common shares were acquired in substantial numbers by arbitrageurs, etc. in 1985 (partly estimated)

Company	Investing Group	Number of shares (tens of thousands)	Share-holding ratio (%)
Fujiya Co. Ltd	Videosellers Group, etc	5,000	~40
Sankyo Seiki Mfg. Co. Ltd	Minebea Group	1,407	18.2
Fuji Spinning Co. Ltd	Sanyo Kosan Group	1,100	10
Nichireki Kagaku	Sanyo Kosan Group	450	20
Gajyoen Kanko K. K.	Sanyo Kosan Group	500	20
Tokai Kogyo Co. Ltd	Hikari Seisakusho Mfg.Co.	2,122	31.5
Morinaga & Co. Ltd	Videosellers Group	2,420	11.1
Kimura Chemical Plant Co. Ltd	Kurosawa Gakkiten	488	23.7
Hokuetsu Paper Mills Ltd	Hokushin Kensetsu Group	1,160	14.4
Jeol Ltd	Hokushin Kensetsu Group	423	6.5
Takasago Perfumery Co. Ltd	Aibi Cosmetics	772	10.0
Kyoei Sangyo Co. Ltd	Korin & Co. Group	518	18.8
Kasho Co. Ltd	Taiyo Kosan Group	210	6.4
Nihon Matai Co. Ltd	Taiyo Kosan Group	210	10.0
3S Shinwa	Sanwa Industries Ltd Group	397	30.0
Nakanogumi Corporation	Daiichi Fudosan Group	200	7.2
Kitano Construction Corporation	Daiichi Fudosan Group	200	6.8

Note: the following companies were transferred from an arbitrageur to another party: Shochiku Co. Ltd, Matsuzakaya Co. Ltd, Toyo Seni, Nippon Lace Co. Ltd, Mitsui Toatsu Chemical Inc., Fujita Kanko, Toyo Bosui, and Mikuro Seisakusho.
Source: Nihon Keizai Shimbun, October 18, 1985

shares directly from one of its major shareholders, the General Corporation (presently known as Fujitsu General). Furukawa successfully purchased 100% of the stock of the Unic Corporation, a leading Japanese manufacturer of mobile cranes, with a 40% share of the domestic market, directly from Unic's previous shareholders (Hanwa Kogyo, Nissho Iwai, and Toshoku).

Table 6.7 Listed companies which failed to comply with the listing requirements in 1988[a]

	Units Number of share- holders needed [b]	Proportion of shares acquired by special share- holders (%)	Major share- acquiring group	Number of share- holdings (tens of thousands)	Share- holding ratio (%)
Tachikawa Corporation	393	750	83	Aichi	315	31.5
Fujii	820	1,100	73	Nihon Saiken Toshi	715	22.5
				Chiyo-Bigen	500	15.7
New Tachikawa Aircraft Co. Ltd	648	750	83	Kita Zipper Mfg. Co. Ltd	100	9.3
Nihon Regulator Co. Ltd	578	750	82	Mitsumura Tsusho Sangyo	180	18.0
Janome Sewing Machine Co. Ltd	1,726	2,000	60	Koshin Ltd	3,100	20.3
				Nanatomi	750	4.9
Mitsui Wharf Co. Ltd	651	750	65	Kenji Corporation	444	28.5

Notes:
[a] The figures for Tachikawa are as of December 1987; those for the other companies are as of March 1988.
[b] The necessary number of shareholders for being listed
Source: Nihon Keizai Shimbun, June 25, 1988

When Misawa Homes acquired Nippon Eternit Pipe in February 1987, it directly purchased the entire 35.3% stake held at that time by Nippon Cement. In March 1987, Misawa Homes also purchased a 29% stake in Ishii Precision Tools, whose shares were listed on the Second Section at Tokyo, from Asahi Diamond: in so doing, Misawa gained virtual control over Ishii and became its largest shareholder.

As these cases indicate, not all of the largest shareholders desire to remain as such: at least some of them may be willing to sell if they receive an attractive offer. American and European potential investors should fully explore this kind of share purchase as a first step toward acquisition.

6.2.5 Acquisitions through hostile tender offers

In Japan there are two types of tender offer; one requires prior notification to the MOF (which, amongst other duties, administers and enforces the securities laws and regulations), while the other does not. Under the terms of the Securities and Exchange Act, as amended, prior notification to the MOF is a prerequisite to making tender offers in order to acquire stock or other securities which are listed or traded on any stock exchange or over-the-counter market in Japan, or which are "registered securities" for the purposes of the Act (securities for which a valid registration statement has been filed under the Act for their sale or offer for sale to the general public). A tender offer to acquire shares issued by any other kind of company requires no such prior action. However, in addition to this statutory notification, when a person, firm, corporation, or any other entity which, for the purposes of the Foreign Exchange and Foreign Trade Control Act (the "FEFT Act"), is not resident in Japan makes a tender offer, a form of prior notification (discussed more fully in Section 7.1) must be made under the

FEFT Act, regardless of whether or not the target company is listed or publicly held.

A tender offer to acquire the shares or other securities of a privately held company does not require prior notification under the terms of the Securities and Exchange Act; nor, by virtue of exemption rules, does a tender offer to acquire less than 10% of a listed or over-the-counter company require prior notification under either the Securities and Exchange Act or the FEFT Act. It should be noted, however, that for the purpose of calculating this threshold value of 10%, all holdings beneficially held by "affiliates" of the investor are considered to be owned by him, in addition to any shares that he may own directly (the definition of "affiliates" will be considered later).

Article 27–6 of the Securities and Exchange Act permits the management of a company which is the target of a tender offer to express their views to its shareholders either by the use of advertisements in the printed news media or by direct mail. In other words, the Act itself envisages friendly, unfriendly, and neutral tender offers.

In Japan, both cash and share-for-share tender offers are permitted, just as they are in the US. Nevertheless, the Japanese share-for-share system needs further explanation. In the strict legal sense, under the terms of the Securities and Exchange Act, a tender offer to acquire the shares of a company in exchange for newly issued additional shares of the organization making the tender offer does not constitute a "share-for-share tender offer," and therefore does not require prior notification. On the other hand, in most cases such a tender offer technically (for the purposes of the Act) constitutes a public sale or public offering and therefore does require a prior filing of a registration statement.

Under current Japanese law, tender offers in exchange for newly issued debt securities of the organization making the offer are not permitted.

In addition, again under current Japanese law, Japanese stock corporations are not allowed to acquire or hold their own shares as treasury shares, except in a few limited cases. Therefore it is virtually impossible for such corporations to make tender offers to acquire shares in another company in exchange for their own treasury shares. However, there are no legal obstacles to prevent foreign corporations from making tender offers in Japan to acquire the shares of Japanese companies in exchange for their own treasury shares. Nevertheless, it should be noted that such an offer may constitute a public sale, or offer for sale, and therefore be subject to the prior registration requirement. Also, from a practical point of view, a share-for-share tender offer of this kind could not attract the attention of Japanese investors unless the shares of the organization making the offer were listed and traded on a stock exchange in Japan.

Technically speaking, a tender offer by a person or company to acquire shares in a Japanese company in exchange for the shares of any other company is permissible under the Act; but once again this may constitute a public sale, or offer for sale, and be subject to the prior registration requirement.

A tender offer by a foreign company to acquire shares in a Japanese company, in exchange for existing convertible bonds issued by itself or by any other company, is also technically permissible; but may again fall foul of the prior registration requirement by constituting a public sale.

The procedural requirements for making a tender offer in Japan are essentially the same as in the US, except that a person making such an offer may have to make prior notification to the MOF at least 11 days before the proposed effective date of the transaction. This can be considered to be the Japanese equivalent of the filing of Schedule 14D in the US: under the terms of the Securities and Exchange Act, no person is allowed to make a tender offer unless or until (i) he has made prior notification to the MOF and (ii) ten days have elapsed since acceptance of that notification by the Minister of Finance. In Japan, however, there is no legal requirement to parallel that of Schedule 13D in the US with respect to tender offers.

Under the terms of the Act, no foreign person, firm, or corporation wishing to make a tender offer in Japan is allowed to make the required prior notification by himself: instead it must be filed via a resident filing agent, either a securities firm (whether Japanese or foreign) that is licensed to do business in Japan, or a Japanese commercial bank. In Japan, the agent authorized to act on behalf of the person or organization making the tender offer is responsible for almost all aspects, including receiving shares of the target company purchased by or on behalf of his client: he also acts as his paying agent. In other words, this one agent does what the depository agent, the soliciting agent, and the dealer manager are expected to do in the US. The person or organization making the offer can, if he chooses, nominate a local bank as the depository agent, separate from his local tender offer agent. The data and information that the tender offerer is required to state in the prior notification are basically the same as those required under Schedule 14D in the US.

When the notification has been accepted by the MOF, the law requires that the person or organization making the offer cannot start buying the target company's shares until a copy of the notification has been served on the target company. Bearing in mind that the notification has to be lodged with the MOF at least 11 days before the tender offer is to become effective, the copy is not usually served until the ninth day after acceptance, thus effectively preventing the target company from preparing defensive action. When the tender offer becomes effective, the person or organization making the offer must publicize it in the newspapers and furnish a copy to the relevant stock exchanges. He must also set the period during which offers to purchase target company shares will remain effective: this must be no shorter than 20 and no longer than 30 days. Additionally, he must set and notify the purchase price, which cannot subsequently be altered. He may attach certain conditions to his offer: for example, he may specify that he will not be under any obligation to buy shares if the aggregate number falls below the quota specified by him within the above set period of time; or that he will be obliged to buy shares only to an extent that he has specified. As in the US, once the tender offer becomes effective the offerer is not allowed to purchase target company shares other than through the tender offer.

No hostile tender offers have ever been made in Japan and (as explained more fully in Section 6.2.8) only two nonhostile tender offers have been experienced to date, neither of which was made with a view to acquisition. One was made for accounting purposes, in an attempt to increase the offerer's holdings in the target company by a sufficient percentage to turn the target company into one of the offerer's consolidated subsidiaries. The other is considered to have been made for administrative, rather than business or acquisition, purposes. It was made in Okinawa to consolidate a number of small local utilities companies into one organization, so that Okinawa's utilities could be administered efficiently when the islands were returned to Japan by the US.

We now consider acquisitions through purchases made directly from the target company: these three types of acquisition all require the cooperation and assistance of the target company.

6.2.6 Purchase of newly issued stock by private placement

Friendly acquisition through the purchase of newly issued stock directly from the target company by private placement (hereafter referred to as "acquisition through private stock placement") is commonplace in Japan. Normally, the management of the target company agree to its being acquired and grant to the acquiring company the right to buy its additional shares. Since the articles of incorporation of most Japanese companies include a clause which denies preemptive rights to the shareholders, companies can issue additional shares whenever they see fit, to whomsoever they like, at whatever price they like, and subject to whatever terms and conditions they think fit. Thus if the acquiring party can obtain the assistance and cooperation of the target company's management, this kind of acquisition is the easiest, quickest, and (from the point of view of maintaining secrecy) most reliable way of achieving his objective. And unless the purchase price (fixed by the board) at which additional shares are issued is unreasonably low, there is little possibility of the acquisition being challenged by other target company shareholders.

This type of acquisition was carried out by Misawa Homes when it acquired Hamano Industries and the Suzuki Iron Works: it acquired 6 million and 5 million additional shares respectively in those two companies, all by private placement. During 1987, there were 24 cases in which listed companies issued additional shares by private placement, and the aggregate share value amounted to ¥111.3 billion. It has been reported that eight of the 24 cases were for acquisition purposes. As was mentioned earlier, no approval or registration is required under the Securities and Exchange Act for any company to grant or issue additional shares to nonshareholding third parties by private placement, or for any person or corporation to purchase additional shares in any other company by private placement. Thus, as long as the acquiring party can obtain the assistance and cooperation of the management of the target company, the acquisition can be accomplished on an almost entirely confidential basis.

American and European businessmen or institutional investors may find it difficult to comprehend how easy it can be in Japan to use private placement as a means of issuing a block of additional shares. In the US or Europe, the issuance of additional shares to a nonshareholding third party would soon be challenged by the existing shareholders. In Japan, however, there are virtually no statutory provisions to protect shareholders' rights and interests against this kind of dilution.

Table 6.8 The difference between the market price and the third party purchase price

Issuer	Acquirer	Purchase price fixed by the board (¥)	Market closing price on the day prior to the day on which the purchase price was fixed (¥)
Mamiya Camera Co. Ltd	Cosmo 80	391	525
Crown Enterprise Ltd	Yunisefu	423	560
Hamano Industries	Misawa Homes	232	478
Suzuki Iron Works	Misawa Homes	240	534
Aiwa	Sony	70	145

Of course, if the board of directors of a company decided to offer additional shares to a particular person, by private place-ment, at an unreasonably favorable price, such a decision would be subject to the approval of the shareholders – and a two-thirds majority would be needed to pass such a special resolution. But what does "unreasonably favorable" mean? If the shares are traded on the stock exchange, their market price can be used as an indicator. Nevertheless, as shown in Table 6.8, there have been many cases in the past in which shares have been allotted and issued by private placement at a price sub-stantially below their market value, without the approval of the existing shareholders. In Table 6.8 is shown a comparison be-tween the purchase price fixed by the board of directors and the market closing price on the day prior to the day on which that price was fixed.

As can be seen from Table 6.8, acquisitions carried out in a spirit of cooperation, through private stock placement, are far less costly to the acquiring parties than acquisitions through purchase on the stock market. Of course, under the terms of the Commercial Code, when an existing shareholder of the target company learns that the company is going to offer additional shares to a third party at an unreasonably low price, without the shareholders' approval, he may challenge the validity of the allotment and seek an injunction. However, because the issue of shares by private stock placement is normally carried out without any form of direct notice to each shareholder, publicity usually being limited to a notice in an official gazette or a newspaper, existing shareholders rarely have sufficient time to file a petition for an injunction. The judicial precedents indicate that if a shareholder's petition is not filed in good time, a Japanese court will probably dismiss the petition in order to protect the "bona fide third party."

The message for American and European potential investors is therefore that acquisition through private stock placement usually affords considerable economic advantages.

6.2.7 Purchase of newly issued convertible bonds

Acquisitions made via the purchase of newly issued convertible bonds directly from the target company, again by means of private placement (hereafter referred to as "acquisitions through private bond placement"), are essentially similar in nature to acquisitions through private stock placement. Again, the target company's board of directors is free to act as it sees fit, as long as the price is not "unreasonably favorable" to the purchaser.

Certain guidelines for the public offering of convertible bonds do exist: they have been jointly established by the MOF and the major securities firms. These guidelines require that when a listed company issues convertible bonds to the general public, their conversion price must be equal to 105% of the average market closing price of the company's common stock during a certain specified period of time immediately prior to the date upon which the conversion price is fixed. However, the guidelines do not apply when bonds are issued by private placement.

Interestingly, this technique was used by Minebea for precisely the opposite reason. When it became the target of Trafalgar's acquisition attempt in 1985, Minebea issued ¥10 billion worth (based on the aggregate par value) of convertible bonds to its second largest shareholder, Keiaisha, and ¥3 billion each to the Sumitomo Trust & Banking Corporation and the Long-Term Credit Bank of Japan Ltd by private placement, in an attempt to defeat Trafalgar. Trafalgar challenged this action through the courts, on the grounds that the purpose of the issue was simply to defeat its attempts, and that conversion of the bonds into common shares would constitute dilution: it sought a declaratory judgment to the effect that the bond issue was null and void. However, in the light of subsequent events, Trafalgar withdrew from the case before any decision was reached.

6.2.8 Friendly tender offers

As mentioned earlier, there have been a couple of friendly tender offers in the past in Japan, cases in which the target company management have assisted and cooperated. One such case (mentioned in Section 6.2.5) involved utility companies in Okinawa. The other, which is probably of greater interest to readers, concerned an American company, the Vendix Corporation.

Vendix originated tender offers in Japan. In 1972 it made a tender offer to purchase shares in the Jidosha Kiki Company: the two companies had enjoyed equity and licensor/licensee relations for many years. At that time Vendix owned 13% of Jidosha Kiki's issued and outstanding shares, and set out to increase its holding to at least 20%, so that it could treat Jidosha Kiki as one of its consolidated subsidiaries (for accounting purposes in the US). As readers might correctly observe, the best way for Vendix – a friendly shareholder – to achieve this objective would have been to ask Jidosha Kiki to issue to Vendix a sufficient number of additional shares by private placement. Vendix did so, but failed because of opposition from other major shareholders. As an alternative course of action, Vendix tried to purchase additional shares on the open market, but there were insufficient shares available. Finally, Vendix resorted to tender offer, attaching to its tender offer a condition that it would not be obliged to buy any more shares beyond the number that would bring its holding up to 20%. Yamaichi Securities was appointed as Vendix's tender offer agent, and Yamaichi representatives visited Jidosha Kiki's shareholders throughout the country in an attempt to solicit selling orders.

The Okinawa case took place in 1975–6. Three utility companies were just too many for Okinawa to support: and the Japanese government considered that the population would benefit if the three companies could somehow be consolidated into one. All three companies had been badly affected by the oil-price crisis, and their individual performances were so poor that rapid amalgamation could not be seen to bring immediate benefits to the shareholders. Furthermore, amalgamation would be confusing for all parties, and difficult to achieve. To enhance the shareholders' interest, and come to a viable arrangement, it was eventually agreed (with the government's advice) that one company, the Okinawa Electric Power Company, would acquire shares in the other two, the Okinawa and the Chuo Power Supply Companies, at a fair market price through tender offer.

Two tender offers were immediately made by the Okinawa Electric Power Company, with Yamaichi Securities, Nihon Kangyo Kakumaru Securities, and Shin Nihon Securities acting as the tender offer agents. Unlike the Vendix case, there were no limits attached this time, and all of the outstanding shares of the two companies were subject to the tender offers. Since the shareholders who agreed to sell were given the right to do so in exchange for the Okinawa Electric Power Company's convertible bonds, these were really exchange tender offers. The shareholders of the two target companies considered that the terms and conditions, particularly the chance to buy convertible bonds, were so attractive that the Okinawa Electric Power Company was able to acquire a full 100% holding in the other two companies, which subsequently merged with it.

These two cases of friendly tender offers, without any positive intention to acquire control, remain unique within Japan. There may be a number of reasons why further tender offers have not come about.

First, there is the traditional Japanese objection to the idea of treating companies as objects of sale and purchase transactions. The Japanese man in the street regards the acquisition of a company through tender offer as something as extreme and unsophisticated as, say, cattle rustling in a wild west movie!

Second, he believes that the purchase of additional shares through private placement is sufficient, and that it is exceptional and unusual for the allotment of such shares to be blocked by other shareholders, as was the case with Vendix.

Third, if a company were to resort to tender offer to acquire control over another company, press announcements would attract the attention of the public and reporters alike, making both companies the prey of the mass media. The acquiring company would probably be accused of being greedy, and bad publicity would mean that business would be lost to competitors, whatever the outcome of the offer itself.

Fourth, tender offers are expensive compared to the gradual covert accumulation of shares on the stock market, or the accumulation of convertible or warrant bonds on overseas markets.

Taking all of these factors into consideration, we may say that tender offers are seen as being the worst possible course of action.

All of these negative attitudes, which invariably apply when one Japanese company acquires another, do not necessarily apply when a foreign investor acquires a Japanese company. However, it must be emphasized that these strongly held and very deep-rooted views will not conveniently vanish in a year or two's time. American and European potential investors are very likely to continue to encounter significant negative reactions from Japanese business circles. One particular episode should be borne in mind.

When Trafalgar visited a number of major Japanese securities firms and announced its intention to make a tender offer to acquire shares in Minebea, it is said that all of them kindly yet firmly turned down Trafalgar's request that they should act as tender offer agents. Trafalgar may not have been well known in Japan, and its real intention – to seek a capital gain rather than to acquire Minebea – may have been suspected from the outset, but the major reason why the companies rejected Trafalgar's requests was that the very idea of hostile tender offers was so repugnant that none of the securities firms approached by Trafalgar were prepared to be the first to participate.

6.2.9 The use of proxy solicitation as leverage

In Japan, as in the US and Europe, it is legal and feasible to use the solicitation of proxies, or proxy battles, as leverage in order to acquire an existing company or business through a merger, or through the purchase of the business or assets. In this section, the procedural requirements under Japanese law will be discussed in detail.

A shareholder who wishes to cause the company to merge with another, or who wishes to remove any members of the board, must first exercise the right of proposal to which he is entitled under the Commercial Code. Under the terms of the Code, a shareholder (acting alone or as part of a group of shareholders) who has continuously owned for at least six months 1% or more of the company's issued and outstanding shares, or a number of shares that is equivalent to 300 Statutory Voting Units – whichever is less – is entitled to propose any action and to vote at a shareholders' meeting, provided that the proposal is furnished in writing at least six weeks before the date of the meeting. He may also request that the proposal should be included in the agenda that is circulated when the shareholders' meeting is announced. In order for the proposal to be passed as a formal resolution, he should solicit proxies from as many other compliant shareholders as possible. In soliciting proxies, he must comply with the "Rules Governing the Solicitation of Proxies in Relation to Listed Shares": these are promulgated under the Securities and Exchange Act and are the Japanese equivalent of the Proxy Rules in the US. Although they are neither so detailed nor so extensive as their US equivalent (Regulation 14A – Solicitation of Proxies) and consist of merely nine sections, they adequately stipulate what a proxy statement must contain.

Having prepared the proxy statement in accordance with these rules, he can then send copies out to other shareholders: a copy must be sent simultaneously to the Director General of the Regional Finance Bureau (a department of the MOF) having jurisdiction over the shareholder or group of shareholders. Needless to say, as in the US and Europe, no one is permitted to circulate a proxy statement that contains any misrepresentation, or which is rendered misleading by the deliberate omission of information.

It is possible to use the proxy statement to make any proposals that could normally be expected to be on the agenda, including, but not limited to, those listed in the rules; that is, proposals for removing board members, appointing new members, amending or modifying the articles of incorporation, merging or being taken over, and allotting new shares to a third party who is not already a shareholder.

In order to solicit proxies in an attempt to acquire a publicly held Japanese company, an American or European investor must first satisfy that 1%/300 Statutory Voting Units criterion. In fact, the more shares he can obtain, the better. If he can obtain a holding of 3% or more, he will be entitled under the Commercial Code to convene a shareholders' meeting, for whatever purpose.

Since an action proposing a merger, or a transfer of all or substantially all of the target company's assets and business, can only be approved by a two-thirds majority of the shareholders – including both those present and those represented at the shareholders' meeting – anyone who holds only 1% to 3% faces an uphill struggle. He must successfully solicit enough proxies to meet this two-thirds requirement; and it may be impossible for anyone holding 50% or less to accomplish this, even with the support of other floating shareholders.

If a merger is proposed, the proxy statement must include the following: a copy of the proposed merger agreement; a written statement of the major terms and conditions of the proposed agreement; and a copy of the financial statement (balance sheet and profit and loss account) of each of the companies involved, for the most recent fiscal year.

Since no foreign company can directly merge with or be taken over by a Japanese company, the only possible way for a foreign company to "merge" is for it to merge indirectly, using its local subsidiary in Japan as a vehicle: the existence of that local subsidiary is an essential prerequisite. On the other hand, if a foreign company acquires the assets of a Japanese company, it need not have any local subsidiary in Japan.

6.2.10 Proxy solicitation to oust or select directors

It goes without saying that equity ownership is not the only way to acquire a company: control of the board of directors confers virtual control of the company. A shareholder who owns a substantial percentage holding and who desires to acquire the company through the solicitation of proxies may, if he so wishes, propose a shareholders' resolution to remove opposing board members and replace them with his own nominees.

As mentioned earlier, the normal period of office for directors in Japan is two years: to remove a director in mid-term a two-thirds majority is again needed at the shareholders' meeting. It is rather easier to wait until the present members' terms expire, as only a simple majority is needed when the board is re-elected. Of course, this may involve waiting for up to two years.

Since few Japanese companies adopt cumulative voting for the election of directors, it is theoretically impossible for a shareholder or group of shareholders to influence the election of their own nominees, let alone control the entire board, unless they have a majority percentage holding. From a practical point of view however, as statistics show, it is very difficult for a company to resist an action proposed by a shareholder who owns a substantial minority percentage holding.

6.2.11 Proxy solicitation to obtain new shares or bonds

It is possible for a shareholder who owns a substantial percentage of a company's shares to use proxy solicitation to increase his holding through the allotment to him of additional shares or convertible bonds, and then to acquire the company using his increased holding as leverage. Ordinarily, the board of directors has the right to allot new shares or bonds to whomsoever it sees fit (subject to the conditions discussed earlier, in Section 6.2.6) and therefore a shareholder who wishes to acquire the company in this way first has to propose two shareholders' resolutions: one to change the company's articles of incorporation so that any allotment of new shares or bonds will require a shareholders' resolution; and the other to allot the necessary number of shares or bonds to him. Of course, if he were to try to persuade the company to allot additional shares or convertible bonds to him at an unreasonably favorable price, the shareholders' approval would be needed in any case, and so no changes in the articles of incorporation would be necessary – but this would again call for a two-thirds majority.

A further word of explanation is needed here in order to understand more fully the right of shareholders to propose shareholders' resolutions. It was not until 1981 that the Commercial Code was amended to introduce such a provision: since then the number of instances in which shareholders have exercised their new rights has increased steadily. Two such cases were reported in 1983: There were three in 1984, three in 1985, four in 1986 – and then at least 15 in the first six months of 1987. It is expected that the use of proxy solicitation coupled with a proposed shareholders' resolution as leverage to acquire a company or business will also increase. In most of the cases reported to date shareholders, with percentage ownerships ranging from 0.01% to about 25%, have exercised the right to propose the removal or appointment of directors, or to propose an increase in dividends – but all such proposals have failed.

Only two of these cases were accompanied by proxy solicitation. In June 1983, Dietman Eitaro Itoyama, who was one of the Yomiuri Land Company's major shareholders, proposed three shareholders' resolutions: One for the election of himself and his nominee as directors of Yomiuri Land; the second for a stock split or stock dividend; and the third for the appointment of a special inspector to inspect Yomiuri Land's books of accounts and financial statements. Then in 1987 the Tomoe Shokai Group, which was the largest shareholder of Nepon, a Tokyo Stock Exchange listed company, proposed two shareholders' resolutions; one calling for the dismissal of the president, who had rejected Tomoe's bid for business association, and the other to increase the cash dividend.

6.2.12 Acquisitions through mergers

An investor who desires to acquire an existing Japanese company can obtain the cooperation of its management in three different ways; by merger, purchase of its business, or purchase of its assets. Each of these is now discussed.

While in the US there are two types of merger, cash mergers and share-for-share (or securities-for-securities) mergers, it should be noted that under Japanese law only share-for-share or stock exchange mergers can take place in Japan. A merger on a cash settlement basis can only be accomplished by buying all of the business and assets of the target company, and then allowing it to be dissolved or liquidated.

In order for a foreign company to acquire a Japanese company through merger, the former must have a Japanese subsidiary, which it must use as its vehicle for the proposed action. A draft merger agreement must be negotiated between the boards of directors of the subsidiary and the target company. When an agreement has been finalized and approved by both boards, it must be signed by and on behalf of both companies, and will become effective subject to the approval of the shareholders: both companies must then convene special shareholders' meetings. At the same time, both companies must notify their creditors of the proposed merger and, in order to protect the latter's rights and interests, give them a reasonable amount of time in which to register their opposition, if any. If any creditors of either company do register opposition within the specified period, the company must either fully repay all outstanding debts that it owes to such creditors or, in lieu of repayment, deposit with a trustee sufficient collateral to cover the repayment.

Under the terms of the Commercial Code, shareholders of either company who object to the proposed merger have the right to demand that the company should purchase shares at a fair market price. Since only share-for-share mergers are permitted, the question of how to fix the ratio at which shares are to be exchanged then becomes of paramount importance. When Kyocera merged with Yashika, a camera manufacturer which was in serious financial trouble, the ratio set was one Kyocera share for 13 of Yashika's.

178

6.2.13 Purchase of the business

The transfer of an existing business is equivalent under Japanese law to what is called "business transfer" in US law. From a legal point of view, there are two types of transfer in Japan. One requires the shareholders' approval in the form of a special resolution (again requiring a two-thirds majority), while the other needs only the approval of the board of directors. The sale or purchase of all, or substantially all, of a company's business constitutes a transfer of the first type. Any sale or purchase of a lesser extent is considered immaterial under the terms of the Commercial Code, and constitutes a transfer of the second type. The sale or transfer by a company of any one of its branch offices, factories, or operating divisions may be considered to constitute a transfer of substantially all of its business, for the purposes of the Commercial Code. However, the difference between the two types is hard to define.

The distinction between what amounts to "substantially all" and what does not is generally made by examining objective factors, such as the ratio between the book value of the part of the business that is subject to the transfer and the book value of the company's total assets; the percentage contribution of that part of the business to the company's total earnings; or the ratio of the number of employees in that part of the company to the total workforce.

From the point of view of labor law, there are two types of business transfer in Japan: one is to inherit and retain the workforce, while the other is not. If the workforce is to be retained, suitable provision must be made in the acquisition agreement, and the acquiring company must enter into negotiation with the workers or their unions about new terms and conditions of employment. If the acquiring company agrees to accept the same working conditions as before, all should proceed smoothly; but if it does not, serious labor problems can be expected. In such a transfer, workers technically leave their old

179

employment and take up a new offer of employment with the acquiring company. Therefore, the workers' previous employment benefits, such as severance pay and pension entitlements, have to be taken into account. It is not common practice in such cases to pay lump sum severance allowances: instead, the acquiring company usually assumes all of the past service liabilities of its predecessor, including those under retirement benefit programs. For the purpose of calculating retirement benefits, employees' past service with their previous employer is normally credited to their service with their new employer. In addition, problems concerning matters such as company accommodation, welfare facilities, medical insurance, and other social benefits have to be discussed and resolved.

Unlike in the case of a merger, in a transfer of an existing business the transferee is not required to assume the liabilities of the transferor, or any part thereof. Even if the transferee agrees to assume all or part of the liabilities, the transferor still remains liable unless he can obtain the consent of his creditors. There are two important points which a transferee should keep in mind.

First, the Commercial Code provides that if a company transfers or assigns its trading name together with its business, then the transferor and transferee become jointly and severally liable for the former's liabilities, unless the transfer is otherwise registered on the Companies Register, or the transferor's creditors are notified of it. Therefore it is best not to acquire the transferor's trading name, unless it brings with it invaluable goodwill.

Second, the Code also provides that the transferee shall be deemed to have assumed the liabilities of the transferor if the transfer is publicly announced through the printed news media or otherwise. The transferee should therefore be careful to avoid any kind of public announcement.

The acquisition of an existing business involves less red tape than a merger, in that there is no statutory waiting period to give creditors a chance to register their opposition.

A final important point about acquiring an existing business is that, under the terms of the Commercial Code, the transferor is automatically prohibited from engaging, either directly or indirectly, in any business which is identical to that which he has just transferred or is about to transfer. It is common practice to include a specific noncompetition clause in business transfer agreements. In the rather cumbersome language of the Code, if the agreement contains such a clause, the transferor will be deemed to have represented, agreed, covenanted, and warranted to the transferee that he shall not engage, either directly or indirectly, in any business which is identical to that which he has just transferred or is about to transfer within the prefecture or prefectures in which he has theretofore, either directly or indirectly, carried on such business, or within any other prefecture or prefectures directly adjoining to any of the aforesaid prefectures, for a period of 30 years following the effective date of the transfer. In the absence of a noncompetition clause in the agreement, the transferor will be deemed to have represented, agreed, covenanted, and warranted to the transferee that he shall not engage, either directly or indirectly, in any business which is identical to that which he has just transferred or is about to transfer within the city or cities in which he has theretofore, either directly or indirectly, carried on such business, or within any other city or cities directly adjoining to any of the aforesaid cities, for a period of 20 years following the effective date of the transfer.

Any transfer or acquisition of an existing business which is subject to the shareholders' approval under the Code is subject to the right of dissenting shareholders to have their shares purchased at a fair market price, as in the case of a merger.

6.2.14 The purchase of assets

The sale or transfer by a company of any of its assets, as distinguished from its business, is not subject to the approval

181

of its shareholders. Therefore neither party has to worry about the solicitation of proxies, or the claims of dissenting shareholders. Nor is it subject to the approval of the board of directors. In most cases, the sale or transfer of assets is within the authority of the chief executive officer of the company who, in the case of a Japanese company, is the Representative Director.

In practice, however, it is difficult to distinguish a transfer of assets from a transfer of business. If a company were to sell or transfer its production equipment or its inventory of merchandise *en bloc*, this would most probably be viewed as a transfer of assets. Similarly, if a company were to sell or transfer its production equipment together with the factory in which the equipment was housed, this would also be considered as a transfer of assets. However, if the company also sold or transferred the factory workforce, the transaction would most probably be regarded as a transfer of business.

If an investor desiring to acquire an existing business in Japan considers that his objective can be achieved by purchasing a specific patent, proprietary technical or engineering information, or a brand name or trademark, all he has to do is to purchase whatever he needs as an assets transfer. He need not purchase or otherwise acquire from the seller any of the latter's business or goodwill. However, if he does purchase or otherwise acquire the goodwill associated with the assets, or trade secrets such as lists of customers or suppliers, then the transaction will probably be regarded as a transfer of business.

The purchase of assets can obviously be accomplished more rapidly, and more confidentially, than the purchase of business. Furthermore, in cases where the transaction is deemed to be an assets purchase, the noncompetition obligation referred to above does not apply, unless the seller and purchaser jointly agree otherwise.

7

The Legal Framework and Tax Implications

7.1 THE FOREIGN EXCHANGE AND FOREIGN TRADE CONTROL ACT

7.1.1 Prior notification

No foreign individual, corporation, or other organization can freely purchase or otherwise acquire shares in a Japanese company except for portfolio investment purposes. The acquisition of shares in order to acquire the company, or to actively participate in its management is, in most cases, subject to the procedural requirements set out in the Foreign Exchange and Foreign Trade Control Act (the "FEFT Act"), as amended.

Some definitions are needed in order to explain how the FEFT Act operates. A "foreign corporation" is defined as a corporation or other entity which is organized under the laws of any jurisdiction other than Japan, or has its principal office in any jurisdiction other than Japan, or which is organized under the laws of Japan but has 50% or more of its shares beneficially owned, either directly or indirectly, by foreign investors. A "foreign investor" is defined as a foreign individual or group of individuals and/or a foreign corporation or group of corporations. A "publicly held Japanese corporation" is defined in the FEFT Act as any listed company or any other company the shares of which are traded on the over-the-counter market.

To: Mr. _____
     The Minister of Finance

     Mr. _____
     The Minister of International
     Trade & Industry

Notifying party	Name or corporate name and name of chief executive officer		
	Residence or location of principal place of business or head office		Nationality
	Occupation or line of business and amount of capital		Paid-up share capital
	Gross annual revenue		Number of employees
	Classification of notifying party The notifying party is: (Mark whichever is applicable.)	☐ (a) an individual who is an exchange non-resident; ☐ (b) a corporation or other entity incorporated under the laws of a foreign country or having its principal place of business in a foreign country; ☐ (c) a corporation of which 50% or more of its shares or equity interests are, directly or indirectly, owned by a person or persons classified in (a) or (b) above; ☐ (d) a corporation or other entity wherein a majority of directors and/or a majority of the executive officers are exchange non-residents; or ☐ (e) acquiring the shares which he or it is going to acquire hereunder on behalf of any other person classified in any of (a) through (d) above.		
	Local filing agent	Name or corporate name and name of chief executive	
		Address or location of head office	
	Place of business contact: and name and telephone number of person in charge		

Figure 7.1 The official form of notification for the proposed acquisition of shares.

1. Issuing company	(1) Name or corporate name and name of chief executive		
	(2) Address or location of head office		
	Telephone number of person in charge		(4) Number of employees	
	(3) Business purposes as stipulated in the articles of incorporation		
	(5) Paid-up share capital (In case of issuance of additional shares, show the amount of share capital after the completion of the issuance.)	Authorized share capital	
		Paid-up share capital	
2. Shares to be acquired	(1) The shares of the issuing company are:	☐ (a) listed on a stock exchange; ☐ (b) traded on the over-the-counter market; or ☐ (c) neither listed on any stock exchange nor traded on the over-the-counter market.	
	(2) Type of allotment or acquisition		
	(3) Class and number of shares to be acquired	• Class: • Number: • Aggregate par value: • Aggregate purchase price: • Notifying party's shareholding percentage after the completion of the proposed acquisition:	

Figure 7.1 (cont.) The official form of notification for the proposed acquisition of shares

185

3. Class, number, and aggregate par value of shares of the same issuing company held by the notifying party at the time of making this notification, if any		• Class: • Number: • Aggregate par value: • Aggregate purchase price: • Notifying party's shareholding percentage before the completion of the proposed acquisition:	
4. Class, Number, and aggregate par value of shares of the same issuing company held by any of the notifying party's "affiliates" (as such term is defined in §2.4 of the Cabinet Order) at the time of making this notification, if any		• Class: • Number: • Aggregate par value: • Aggregate purchase price: • Such affiliate's shareholding percentage:	
5. Selling party	(1) Name or corporate name and name of chief executive		
	(2) Address or location of head office		
	(3) Number of shares to be sold and their selling price		
6. Broker involved	(1) Name or corporate name and name of chief executive		
	(2) Address or location of head office		
	(3) Occupation or major line of business		
7. Proposed closing date			

Figure 7.1 (cont.) The official form of notification for the proposed acquisition of shares

8. Proposed date of payment of purchase price	
9. Manner of payment	☐ (a) Payment will be made by "Standard Method of Payment"; or ☐ (b) Payment will be made by other means of payment. (Please specify.)
10. The purpose which the notifying party wants to achieve by the proposed purchase of shares	
11. Issuing company's production and marketing plans	
12. Issuing company's directors and major shareholders	
13. Remarks	

Date of acceptance
Acceptance no.

Figure 7.1 (cont.) The official form of notification for the proposed acquisition of shares

Then, when a foreign individual or a foreign corporation purchases or otherwise acquires (i) a share or shares in a privately held Japanese company, or (ii) shares in a publicly held Japanese corporation that result in the foreign investor owning at least 10% of the issued and outstanding shares of that company, he must comply with the prior notification requirement set out in the FEFT Act.

For the purposes of the Act, shares of a Japanese company which are owned by an "affiliate" of a foreign investor are deemed to be beneficially owned by the foreign investor. In this context, "affiliate" means (i) any company which controls, is controlled by, or is virtually under the control of, a foreign investor, (ii) any individual who is the spouse or a direct lineal descendant of a foreign investor, (iii) any other person who is a director or officer of a foreign investor or any of his affiliates (see (i) above), or (iv) any company that has a majority of directors or officers who are such persons.

The terms "control," "controlled," and "controlling," as used in connection with the definition of "affiliate," mean the ownership, whether direct or indirect, of 50% or more of the shares or other proprietary interest in the affiliate, or the right to elect a majority of the board members.

What all this means in effect is that, theoretically, if a foreign individual and his brothers and sisters, or two or more unaffiliated foreign corporations, each acquired 9.9% of the issued and outstanding shares of a publicly held Japanese company, they would not be required to comply with the prior notification requirement of the Act. However, this is something about which the author is not certain, as there is still some ambiguity in the Act, and so care is needed. If any individual foreign investor were to increase his holding to 10% or more, he would then have to comply with the prior notification requirement. If a foreign investor were to use a Japanese individual or company as his nominee in acquiring shares in a Japanese corporation, whether or not his intention was to circumvent the requirement, the shares acquired and held by the nominee would be considered to be beneficially owned by the foreign investor, and prior notification would still be unavoidable if his holding were to reach or exceed 10%.

If prior notification becomes necessary, it must be made through the Bank of Japan to the Minister of Finance, and to other ministers having jurisdiction over the Japanese company concerned. The written notification must contain, amongst other information, the investor's name and address, the purpose of the purchase or acquisition, the purchase price or acquisition cost, the expected date of purchase or acquisition, and the name, address, and capitalization of the Japanese company. An English translation of the form in which the notification must be filed is shown in Figure 7.1.

7.1.2 The waiting period

Under the terms of the Act, a foreign investor will generally not be allowed to complete the proposed purchase or acquisition until 30 days after the date of acceptance of the prior notification by the Minister of Finance and his government colleagues. This is a maximum period, and the actual waiting time may sometimes be less than 30 days. The waiting period is currently either partially or totally waived in certain industries, according to the official notice entitled "Designation by the Minister of Finance and Other Relevant Ministers of Industries for the Enforcement of the Joint Ministerial Ordinance Concerning Direct Investment in Japan." The 30-day period is currently totally waived in the construction, bakery, transportation, and communications industries, in the retail and restaurant trades, in the financial sector, including insurance, in real estate, and in all other kinds of service industry. The waiting period has currently been shortened to two weeks in the following industries: the manufacture of cheese, biological preparations, explosives, and nuclear fuel; the aircraft, arms, nuclear energy, space, and bus transportation industries; oil storage and retailing, LPG filling, and LPG storage.

As a consequence of the reservations to which Japan is entitled under the OECD Treaty, in December 1980 the Japanese government publicly announced, in the form of a resolution of the Ministerial Council, that all proposed purchases or acquisitions by foreign investors in the following industrial sectors should be carefully reviewed by the government for the time being: agriculture, forestry, fishing, mining, petroleum, leather and hide processing, and the manufacture of leather products. This resolution is still in effect, and it remains very difficult, if not completely impossible, for a foreign investor to purchase or acquire shares in a Japanese company that is involved in any of the above industrial sectors, whether or not this activity is the primary business of the company.

The Minister of Finance and his relevant colleagues are entitled to extend the waiting period from 30 days to as much as four months if they have reason to believe that the proposed purchase or acquisition: could have adverse effects on Japan's national security, public order, or public safety; or could have substantial adverse effects on the operations of the Japanese company's competitors, or on the sound operation and development of the Japanese economy itself; or might breach the principle of reciprocity of direct foreign investment between Japan and the foreign investor's country of origin, should that country be one with which Japan has no international treaty or convention.

A further extension of the period to five months is possible if the Minister of Finance and his colleagues decide to seek the opinion of the Foreign Exchange Council. If the Council's response is negative, the investor may be recommended to modify or even abandon his proposed purchase or acquisition, depending on the circumstances. And should the investor fail to comply with such a recommendation, the government will order him to do so.

No compliance orders have actually been issued to date, but delaying tactics have been put into effect. Trafalgar's application to the Minister of Finance and the Minister of International Trade and Industry in February 1986, in connection with its proposed purchase of more than 10% of the issued and outstanding shares of Minebea, led to a government order that Trafalgar must wait for the full 30-day period, contradicting the total or partial waivers set out above.

7.1.3 Katakura Industries vs. a Hong Kong investor

What would the consequences be under private law, including the law of contract, if a foreign investor were to purchase or acquire shares in a Japanese company in violation of the FEFT Act; that is, without filing a prior notification? Under the terms of the Commercial Code or the law of contract, would the transaction be regarded as invalid? This is a very interesting legal issue, which has been much discussed in business and legal circles. In the event of noncompliance by a foreign investor, not only that investor but also any Japanese individual or organization who may have aided him in his attempt to avoid compliance could face a prison sentence of up to three years, or could be fined up to ¥1,000,000. Obviously, a fine is the only option available if the foreign investor is a corporation. However, it is unrealistic to expect that the statutory fine will deter violations of the Act. The current academic opinion is that new legislation should be introduced so that purchases or acquisitions made in violation of the FEFT Act can be rendered null and void. However, the government does not as yet share this view.

The government's view, expressed in an answer to a complaint filed against it in the Tokyo District Court in 1981, is very important. The plaintiff, a foreign investor based in Hong Kong, had already purchased a substantial percentage of shares in Katakura Industries Co. Ltd, a listed company engaged primarily in the textile business. He then attempted to buy additional shares, and accordingly filed a prior notification with the government, in anticipation of early acceptance. However, in an obvious attempt to prevent acquisitions by foreign investors, in November 1980 the government published a list of companies that would be subject to "careful review" should a foreign investor acquire a shareholding of 25% or more – Katakura was included on this list. (At that time the Act was enforced in a more protectionist manner than is now the case: the list included Sankyo, a pharmaceutical company, Arabian Oil, Fuji Electric, a parent company of Fujitsu, Hitachi, Tokyo Keiki, a manufacturer of aviation and navigation instruments as well as hydraulic equipment, General Oil, Showa Oil, Mitsubishi Oil, Toa Oil, and Koa Oil.) As a result of Katakura's inclusion, the plaintiff was effectively prevented from purchasing additional shares in the company. Therefore, in February 1981 he instituted an action against the Japanese government, seeking a court order to cancel Katakura's inclusion on the list on the grounds that the government's action had no proper legal foundation.

In its defense, the government stated that the validity and enforceability under private law of a contract for the purchase or acquisition of shares in a Japanese company by a foreign investor, in violation of the prior notification requirement under the Act, "should not necessarily be denied."

This means that the acquisition itself could remain fully valid and enforceable, from the point of view of both parties, unless the Japanese company had a specific provision in its articles of incorporation, or rules governing the transfer of shares, authorizing the company to reject any request for a transfer of ownership of shares acquired in violation of the Act. In other words, even if the acquisition was illegal under the Act it could still be accomplished as long as the foreign investor was willing to pay the legal penalty.

However, it would be unwise to take risks and assume that the requirement can be disregarded: it is always possible that an action could be brought, and the transaction declared null and void, under private law on the grounds that public order or the policy of the Civil Code has been violated.

Apart from the outcome of this legal debate, it is expected that as a practical measure to prevent such illegal transactions the government – and particularly the MOF – is increasingly likely to contact all of the securities firms and advise them not to accept purchase orders from the foreign investor in question. The securities firms will undoubtedly follow the government's advice, and the foreign investor will have no option but to forgo the purchase.

7.2 ANTIMONOPOLY IMPLICATIONS OF MERGERS AND ACQUISITIONS

7.2.1 Prohibition of holding companies

The Antimonopoly Act, as amended, provides that no person may organize a holding company, or cause one to be set up, and that no existing company may act as a holding company. These prohibitions apply equally to foreign individuals and corporations who do business in Japan. Before World War II, Japan was unique among the industrialized capitalist countries because its economic and industrial structure was under the unusually strong oligopolistic control of a small number of *zaibatsu* groups. The statutory prohibition of holding companies was introduced as a postwar measure to prevent the *zaibatsu* groups from reforming.

Under the Act, a "holding company" is defined as one whose primary business purpose is to control another company or other companies in Japan through stock or equity ownership. American and European readers may be very surprised to learn that venture capital companies in Japan are prohibited, by an administrative instruction issued by the Fair Trade Commission (FTC) in order to enforce the prohibition of holding companies, from having seats on the boards of the venture businesses of which they are either shareholders or creditors. The FTC is the independent agency in charge of the administration and enforcement of the Act. Another FTC instruction prohibits venture capital companies from acquiring or holding more than 49% of the shares of any venture business.

While holding companies are prohibited in Japan, it may be possible for a foreign investor to organize or own a Japanese company and use it as a vehicle in order to merge with or acquire another company or other companies in Japan, provided that any company acting as a vehicle only does so for a relatively short period of time.

7.2.2 Prohibition of share ownership that may harm competition

The Antimonopoly Act also provides that no person or corporation may acquire or hold shares in any other corporation if, or to the extent that, this acquisition or holding causes substantial damage to competition in any particular market or market sector. Furthermore, no person or corporation may acquire or hold shares in any other corporation through unfair trade practices: this provision is equivalent to Section 7.1 of the Clayton Act in the US. The term "unfair trade practices" includes offering an unreasonably high purchase price in an attempt to buy all of the available shares of a target company, or launching a boycott of the products or services of a target company in an attempt to damage that company's financial position to such an extent that share acquisition becomes easier.

Here one again encounters a legal dilemma. In antimonopoly cases, the Japanese courts of law have in the past held that such transactions, if completed, are still valid and enforceable under private law or the law of contract, despite their illegality under the Antimonopoly Act. Nevertheless, such illegal transactions are still very risky, because the FTC has the authority to order a person or corporation who has acquired shares in violation of the Act to divest himself or itself of them. Furthermore, as was the case with FEFT Act violations, it is always possible that a transaction could be declared null and void under private law, on the grounds that public order or the policy of the Civil Code has been violated.

There is one material difference between violations of the FEFT Act and those of the Antimonopoly Act. While under the Antimonopoly Act a person or corporation whose illegal share transactions have violated the Act (perhaps creating a state of monopoly and thereby disadvantaging others unfairly) is strictly liable for damages, no such liability arises under the FEFT Act.

Although the FTC is not as active or as strict in enforcing the statutory prohibition of illegal share transactions under the Antimonopoly Act as its American counterparts, the Federal Trade Commission and the Department of Justice, are in enforcing the similar prohibitions set out in the Sherman Act and the Clayton Act, this does not mean that the FTC has never invoked its power of statutory prohibition. In fact, it has done so several times.

In 1950, when the Nippon Oil Company acquired 35% of the Japan Oil Transportation Company, the FTC initiated proceedings against Nippon Oil because the equity relationship between the two companies would result in substantial damage to competition in the oil transportation industry. The case was settled by consent decree, whereby Nippon Oil was forced to divest itself of its entire holdings in Japan Oil Transportation. In 1957, the FTC initiated proceedings against the Yamaha Corporation in connection with Yamaha's ownership of shares in the Kawai Musical Instruments Company, one of Yamaha's direct competitors: at the time, Yamaha owned 24.5% of Kawai. The FTC considered that Yamaha's indirect equity relationship with Kawai was substantially harming competition in the market. This case was also settled by consent decree, whereby

Yamaha was forced to reduce its ownership in Kawai from 24.5% to 9.5%. In 1972 the FTC again initiated proceedings, this time against the Hiroshima Electric Railways Company when it acquired 84.6% of the Hiroshima Bus Company, one of its competitors. This action was again brought on the grounds that competition in the industry would be harmed substantially. The case was again settled by consent decree, the railway company having to reduce its ownership in the bus company to 19.2%, and to abandon entirely its representation on the latter's board of directors. Also in 1972, the FTC initiated proceedings against the Toyo Can Manufacturing Company on the grounds that its ownership in the Hokkaido Can Manufacturing Company would substantially harm competition in the industry: Toyo owned 28.9% of Hokkaido at the time. Another consent decree settlement took place and, following the FTC's recommendations, Toyo reduced its holdings in Hokkaido to 5% and agreed not to involve itself in any way with Hokkaido's management, operations, or personnel matters.

When a foreign corporation which already has a business presence in Japan directly or indirectly acquires a Japanese business or company which is one of its competitors, it must be very careful about the antimonopoly implications: prior informal consultation with the FTC is recommended.

Under the Antimonopoly Act, all foreign corporations (except "financial institutions," as discussed below) that hold shares in Japanese companies must file annual shareholding reports with the FTC. This is a *post facto* reporting requirement, and is therefore different from the prior reporting requirement under the Hart–Scott–Rodino Antitrust Improvement Act of the US.

7.2.3 Restrictions on shareholdings of financial institutions

The Antimonopoly Act places certain restrictions on the shareholdings of financial institutions. No corporation engaged in the financial business is permitted to acquire or hold shares in any other Japanese corporation in excess of 5% of the issued and outstanding shares: this limit is increased to 10% for corporations engaged in insurance. These restrictions were introduced in order to prevent Japan's industries from being controlled by financial institutions, and they apply equally to foreign corporations engaged in the financial or insurance business.

The term "financial business," as defined by the Act, encompasses the businesses of banking (including that defined under the Mutual Banking Act), trust banking, insurance, mutual financing, and securities. Accordingly any corporations, whether Japanese or not, that are engaged in other forms of financial activity are not subject to the above restrictions. It is not easy to define "banking," "trust banking," "mutual financing," or "securities." If foreign potential investors are in any doubt, they must consult experienced Japanese lawyers beforehand.

The term "banking business" is best defined in the Banking Act, as the business of accepting savings or time deposits, and extending loans or discounting notes, or acting as a money exchanger. This means that activities such as the lending of money, the extension of mortgage loans, or leasing are not considered to be "banking," unless they accompany the acceptance of savings or deposits.

Finally, the term "securities business" is best defined in the Securities and Exchange Act, where it is considered to include the following activities: acting as securities dealers or brokers; acting as introducing brokers or agents in connection with the sale or purchase of securities; acting as intermediaries introducing brokers or agents, in connection with sale or purchase transactions involving securities, executed on a securities market; acting as underwriters of securities; and acting as distributors of securities in the primary or secondary markets, or distribution agents of securities in the secondary market. For the purposes of the Antimonopoly Act, what is generally termed an "investment bank" in the US or Europe is regarded as a corporation engaged in the "securities business."

There are certain exemptions from the shareholding restrictions under the Act. First, a corporation engaged in the financial business (hereafter called a "financial institution") may be able to obtain approval from the FTC to increase its shareholding in a Japanese company beyond the normally applicable limit.

Second, a financial institution may hold shares in any Japanese company in excess of the normal limit if such shares have been acquired as a result of the foreclosure of any collateral, or in accordance with an accord and satisfaction. Third, a financial institution engaged in the securities business may freely acquire and hold shares in any other company as portfolio securities in excess of the normal limit. In both of these eventualities, the FTC's approval is needed if shares in excess of the 5% limit acquired in these two ways are held for more than a year.

Fourth, a financial institution may freely acquire and hold shares in any other company in excess of the normal limit as a trustee, under a trust agreement, provided that the beneficiaries of the trust are given the right to exercise the voting rights attached to such shares, or the right to give the trustee appropriate voting instructions.

7.2.4 Restrictions on interlocking directorships

Under the terms of the Antimonopoly Act, no officer or employee of any company may concurrently serve as an officer of any other company if that concurrent service has the effect of substantially harming competition in a specific market: in that event he must resign from one post. The Act also prohibits a company from forcing one of its own nominees onto a competitor, as an officer or employee, through the use of unfair trade practices. Furthermore, if an officer or employee of one company concurrently serves with any of its competitors, and the total assets value of either of the two companies exceeds

¥2 billion, then the first company must notify the FTC of his appointment as an officer of the second company within 30 days following the effective date of the appointment. The above prohibitions and statutory notifications apply equally to foreign corporations doing business in Japan.

The term "officer" as used here includes a member of the board of directors, a corporate officer (as used in Anglo-American corporate law) and, perhaps, a general partner of a partnership organized and already in existence under Anglo-American partnership law.

If a company substantially harms competition in any specific market, unduly restrains trade, or commits any unfair trade practice through interlocking directorships etc., in violation of the prohibitions and notification requirements set out above, and thereby causes damage to a third party, that company will be strictly liable for damages.

During the immediate postwar years, there were quite a few cases in which the FTC invoked the above prohibitions. One particular case, in 1949, involved the Tosa Electric Railways Company. At the time, Tosa had seats on the boards of directors of several of its competitors, including a bus company and a marine transportation company: the FTC ordered Tosa to relinquish these seats entirely on the grounds that the situation violated the prohibitions. Similarly, in 1972, the FTC ordered the Hiroshima Electric Railways Company to relinquish its seats on the board of directors of the Hiroshima Bus Company for the same reason.

7.2.5 Restrictions on shareholdings of entities other than corporations

The Antimonopoly Act also prohibits any individual or other entity (other than a corporation), whether Japanese or foreign, from acquiring or holding shares in a Japanese company if, and to the extent that, competition in any specific market is likely to be substantially harmed as a result.

Further, any individual or other entity (other than a corporation), whether Japanese or foreign, who acquires or holds shares in two or more competing companies in Japan, in excess of 10% of their issued and outstanding shares, must notify the FTC of the acquisition or holding within 30 days.

The term "entity" as used here includes nonprofit-making corporations, mutual insurance companies, partnerships, unions, associations, foundations, and institutions.

7.2.6 Restrictions on mergers

As mentioned earlier, no foreign corporation can merge with, or be merged into, a Japanese corporation. Therefore a foreign corporation seeking to acquire a Japanese corporation through merger must have, or must establish, a subsidiary in Japan which can act as its vehicle. When a subsidiary merges with a Japanese company, it becomes subject to the restrictions on mergers provided for in the Antimonopoly Act.

Under the terms of the Act, two or more companies are prohibited from merging together (i) if competition in a specific market is likely to be substantially harmed as a result, or (ii) if the merger is to be carried out by means of an unfair trade practice.

Furthermore, any corporation merging with any other company that is then dissolved must make prior notification to the FTC, and the merger cannot take effect until the expiration of 30 days following the FTC's receipt of the notification. This 30-day period may be extended to 60 days if the FTC considers it necessary to do so. This waiting period gives the FTC the opportunity to issue a recommendation to the notifying company, or to initiate proceedings if it objects to the merger. However, unless the notifying company has made a material misrepresentation in its notification, the FTC can take no further action after the waiting period has elapsed.

It seems that these restrictions have not always been enforced as strictly as they would be in the US, and there are a number of cases that support this view. For example, in 1958 Yukijirushi Dairy Products successfully merged with Clover Dairy Products without any FTC objections at all, and became the nation's largest supplier of cheese and butter, with 79% and 56% shares of the two markets respectively. Similarly, in 1959 Chuo Fiber and Textiles successfully merged with Teikoku Hemp, becoming the nation's largest supplier of hemp yarn, with a market share of 44.8%. In 1963, New Mitsubishi Heavy Industries, Mitsubishi Nihon Heavy Industries, and Mitsubishi Shipbuilding successfully merged to form what is now the Mitsubishi Heavy Industries Corporation. This merger, although much criticized for allowing the possible revival of the old Mitsubishi Zaibatsu Group, encountered no significant opposition from the FTC. Mitsubishi Heavy Industries became the nation's largest and most diversified heavy industrial company, with a 63% share of the market for paper manufacturing machinery and more than a 25% share of 16 other machinery markets, including that for utilities boilers.

Then came the most controversial merger in the world's antitrust history: Fuji Steel and Yawata Steel merged successfully into what is now the Nippon Steel Corporation. The merger was subject only to some relatively minor conditions placed upon it by the FTC, and the resulting new corporation became one of the world's largest steel manufacturers (second only to the US Steel Corporation), with an incredible 94.2% share of the domestic steel plate market, 87.2% of the domestic rail market, and almost 50% of a number of other domestic steel-related markets. Nippon Steel is now the world's largest steel manufacturing corporation.

7.2.7 Restrictions on the purchase of business or assets

When a foreign company acquires all, or substantially all, of the business or assets of a Japanese company, it is again subject to certain restrictions laid down by the Antimonopoly Act.

Furthermore, it is also subject to the restrictions discussed above with reference to mergers when, as lessee, it "leases all or substantially all of the business" of a Japanese company, or when it acts as manager or trustee, or enters into a contract with a Japanese company for equal sharing of their entire operational profit and loss.

What is important here is that the acquisition, purchase or leasing of *assets* is also subject to the restrictions. As used here, "the lease of all or substantially all of the business" of a Japanese company means also "the lease of all of the business assets" of the company.

There have been relatively few cases in which the FTC has invoked the restrictions in connection with the purchase, acquisition, or leasing of business or assets. One notable case involved the Toho Corporation, one of Japan's leading motion picture companies. In 1950 when Toho, as lessee, leased movie theaters from other companies, the FTC prohibited such leases on the grounds that competition in certain sectors of the movie theater market would be substantially harmed.

Foreign investors, corporations, businessmen, and lawyers who wish to learn more about how the FTC enforces the restrictions under the Antimonopoly Act in connection with acquisitions and holdings of shares, and with mergers, are recommended to study the FTC's own publications entitled "Guidelines for Antimonopoly Review of Acquisitions and Holdings of Shares" and "Guidelines for Antimonopoly Review of Mergers and Acquisitions."

7.3 TAX IMPLICATIONS OF THE ACQUISITION OF JAPANESE COMPANIES BY FOREIGN CORPORATIONS

To avoid exposure to unexpected tax liabilities in connection with, or as a result of, the acquisition of a Japanese company, potential foreign investors must draw up their plans very carefully, with the assistance of licensed Japanese tax consultants and/or certified public accountants (CPAs). Licensed tax consultants are unique to Japan, and must pass national examinations in order to be allowed to practise. While the work of the CPA is oriented very much toward financial audit, the licensed tax consultant focuses on tax advice and consultation services. Also, while CPAs are qualified to do whatever tax consultants do, the same is not true the other way round – tax consultants cannot provide audit services.

It is very difficult to find tax consultants who are experienced in international transactions. By far the safest and quickest way to obtain reliable good advice is to retain the services of one of the major local public accountancy firms, or of one of the "Big Eight" US accountancy firms that do business in Japan.

In this section, the tax implications of the acquisition of a Japanese company or business by a foreign corporation will be briefly discussed. Three kinds of acquisition will be considered: (i) through stock purchases; (ii) through the purchase of existing businesses; and (iii) through merger. Readers should bear in mind, however, that the following discussion is only a very cursory overview of the possible implications, and that serious potential investors should consult with the licensed tax consultants and /or CPAs referred to above.

7.3.1 Acquisition through the purchase of shares

In this case there are no particular tax problems that potential foreign investors need worry about. However, in order to draw up workable acquisition plans, a better knowledge is needed of the problems that Japanese individuals or corporations face when they sell their shares.

First, when a person, corporation, or other entity, whether Japanese or foreign, sells equity securities or debt securities such as shares or bonds in Japan, *securities transfer tax* must be paid. This tax is levied at the rate of 0.55% of the selling price, and is payable on the day of business immediately following that on which the transaction takes place.

Second, *capital gains tax* must be explained, in somewhat greater detail. To simplify matters, consider the example of an unlisted Japanese company, the president and chairman of the board of which is also the largest shareholder. Now suppose that a foreign corporation purchases his entire holding, in an attempt to acquire the company. His sale to the foreign corporation will constitute a taxable securities transfer, and he will become liable for very heavy capital gains tax, if either of the following conditions apply:

1 (a) He owns, or has owned at any time during the immediately preceding three-year period, 30% or more of the issued and outstanding shares of the company (the 30% includes any shares owned by his immediate relatives, including his wife). (b) He sells to the foreign corporation, or to any other party, 5% or more of the then issued and outstanding shares of the company in the same tax year in which the sale to the foreign corporation occurs. (c) During the immediately preceding three-year period, he has sold in aggregate 15% or more of the issued and outstanding shares of the company.

2 During the tax year in which he sells his shares to the foreign corporation, he sells or purchases at least 120,000 shares of the company's stock. (The figure of 120,000 is based on the assumption that the shares have a par value of ¥50. If the value is higher or lower, the figure should be adjusted accordingly.)

Thus, from the seller's point of view, it is very important to determine whether or not the sale constitutes a taxable securities transfer. In order to sell a substantial number of shares and avoid liability, he should sell his shares in a number of transactions; less than 15% in the first year, and less than 5% in each of the subsequent years. If he is the 100% owner, and the foreign corporation wants to acquire a 100% holding, this series of transactions will take many years to accomplish. Naturally, the owner will want to avoid tax liability, and the foreign corporation will want to press on as quickly as possible: therefore acquisition negotiations of this nature often become deadlocked. The real problem hinges upon who should pay the capital gains tax bill: the seller or the foreign corporation; or both; and if both, in what ratio. Consultation with an experienced local tax expert is vital when acquisition plans are being drawn up; to enable the one party to acquire the controlling interest in the company as quickly as possible, while avoiding or minimizing the tax liability of the other party.

One possible approach is to have the Japanese company issue additional shares to the foreign corporation by private placement, so as to reduce the seller's original holding to below 30% before further shares are sold. Another possibility is for the Japanese company to issue convertible bonds, for subsequent transfer to the foreign corporation, which can then exercise its right to convert them into common stock of the Japanese company. Under current Japanese law, a capital gain realized from the sale of convertible bonds is exempt from capital gains tax.

Unfortunately, no matter how carefully a transaction is constructed legally to avoid or reduce capital gains tax, the tax authorities still have the power to reject the transaction, as a scheme illegally drawn up to evade fiscal liabilities. Therefore, both parties must be very careful and, if in any doubt, should contact the tax authorities for a ruling.

Capital gains tax liabilities can sometimes be huge, and can make or break an attempted acquisition. If the seller wants to sell his company and retire, it may be a good idea for him to arrange for the company to pay him a substantial lump sum retirement allowance. This might provide an incentive to sell the shares, because the tax rate applicable to retirement allowances is lower than that applicable to capital gains.

Finally, it should be noted that when a corporation sells shares in another corporation and realizes a net capital gain, this capital gain must be included in the corporation's net earnings, and then becomes subject to corporate tax.

7.3.2 Acquisition of existing businesses

When a Japanese company sells all or part of its business at a profit, it is subject to tax, the burden of which may be very heavy. In such cases, the profit and loss are calculated with respect to each item of the business assets that is included in the sale.

If fixed assets, inventories, and/or securities are sold as part of the sale of a business, the difference between the selling price and their book value is considered to be a capital gain, and will be taxed accordingly. It should be noted that if the selling price is *less* than the fair market value, the difference between the two will also be taxed. Thus, if the fixed assets include land, the selling price should reflect its current market value.

If the company's goodwill is also sold, its entire selling price will be considered as a capital gain, and will be subject to tax. Proceeds from the sale of accounts receivable are not taxed, as long as they are sold at their book value.

The immediate problem faced by a foreign corporation that has purchased an existing business from a Japanese company is how to show the assets it has purchased on its balance sheet. If the foreign corporation makes use of its subsidiary in Japan to complete the transaction, the purchased assets should be shown on the subsidiary's balance sheet, in accordance with the accounting principles that are generally accepted in Japan. In that event, they should be shown on a cost basis. If an asset is purchased at less than its fair market value, the difference will be taxed as a corporate profit.

In the case of the purchase by a foreign corporation of shares in a Japanese company, or of an existing business in Japan, both parties should refer to the tax treaty between Japan and the relevant foreign country so as to avoid any unnecessary tax liabilities.

7.3.3 Tax implications of mergers

In the event of a merger, if the surviving corporation makes a capital gain, this will be taxed. The gain is calculated as the positive balance of the net book value of the dissolving corporation's assets less the price paid to that corporation's shareholders (the amount that the surviving corporation's capital stock will have increased as a result of the merger plus the amount of cash payments, if any, made by it to the shareholders of the dissolving corporation). On the other hand, if the price paid by the surviving corporation for the net assets of the dissolving corporation (the amount of the surviving corporation's capital stock will have increased as a result of the merger plus the amount of cash payments, if any, made by the surviving corporation to the shareholders of the dissolving corporation) exceeds the value shown on the dissolving corporation's own balance sheet, the excess portion will be considered as a liquidation profit and will be subject to tax.

It is common practice, however, for the dissolving corporation to increase or decrease its capital, and/or divest itself of some of its business, before the completion of the merger, in order to carefully adjust the ratio at which its shares are to be exchanged for those of the surviving corporation, so that it will realize no capital gain.

If the aggregate amount of the fair market value of the shares of the surviving corporation issued and delivered to shareholders of the dissolving corporation upon merger in exchange for their shares in the dissolving corporation plus the amount of the cash payment, if any, received by them from the surviving corporation as a result of the merger exceeds the cost to them of their shares in the dissolving corporation, the excess portion will be considered as a liquidation dividend for tax purposes and will, therefore, be subject to income tax, if the shareholders are individuals. If a shareholder is a corporation, it will be allowed to deduct any such liquidation dividend from its taxable income.

In the case of a merger, it is common accounting practice for the surviving corporation to accept the assets of the dissolving corporation at the book value shown on the dissolving corporation's books. It should be noted, however, that the surviving corporation is not allowed to succeed to or inherit tax losses carried over by the dissolving corporation.

8

Post-acquisition Management

It is generally true to say that members of law firms, such as the present author, are not really competent to give advice on the technical aspects of the post-acquisition management of an acquired company. However, it is possible to give various hints and a certain amount of practical advice on some general aspects, as follows.

8.1 RETAIN MOST OF THE EXISTING MANAGEMENT TEAM

As mentioned earlier, in Japan labor and management both believe strongly that companies belong to them – as much as, or more than, they belong to the shareholders. In other words, labor and management consider that they are bound together by a common destiny, and these feelings can be taken advantage of to stimulate the loyalty and motivation of the employees of an acquired company. Even if an American or European corporation successfully acquires a majority interest in a Japanese company, it should not be too eager to remove existing board members and second its own personnel to replace them. It is important to maintain loyalty and sustain morale by avoiding the impression that the acquired company has been "conquered" or "occupied."

8.2 REMEMBER THAT LAYOFF IS UNCOMMON IN JAPAN

In the US it is not uncommon for excess labor to be laid off after an acquisition. In Japan, however, this type of layoff is prohibited by the labor relations laws. American and European corporations must realize that when one Japanese company acquires another, the former invariably guarantees the continuing employment of the latter's employees, under the same terms and conditions as before. For most Japanese employees, acquisition is a once-in-a-lifetime experience. Few of these employees would take advantage of the situation to bargain for improved terms and conditions, or leave the company because the management have refused their requests.

8.3 CULTIVATE A LONG-TERM PERSPECTIVE

The Japanese tend to have a longer-term business and economic perspective than the Europeans and the Americans: Japanese management and labor tend to pursue long-term goals, whereas their European and, particularly, American counterparts tend to favor short-term thinking, as far as the growth and success of their companies are concerned. While Americans and Europeans may be focusing on the improvement of sales and per share net earnings in the near future, their Japanese counterparts may be looking five to ten years ahead.

If an American or European corporation were to acquire a Japanese company and then try to enforce its usual style of management, this could result in the laying off of part of the workforce, or the sale of unprofitable divisions, in order to achieve short-term success. Any action of this kind would result in a serious labor dispute between management and employees in the affected parts of the acquired company, and a dispute of this nature might well develop into an irreconcilable and emotional conflict between the acquired company's employees and its new shareholder – the acquiring company. This, of course, would lead to serious deleterious consequences for the management and operation of the acquired company.

American and European potential investors must bear in mind that, in the worst analysis, they might be required to put in ten times as much time and effort to restore an unprofitable Japanese company to profitability – or progress from marginal to high profitability – as they would in the West.

8.4 STUDY THE JAPANESE COST REDUCTION FORMULA

While America laid off a substantial portion of its national workforce to overcome the depression caused by the 1973 oil-price crisis, Japan came through the same experience with virtually no layoffs. In recent times, Japan's economy has been hit hard by the sharp appreciation of the yen, but layoffs have again been avoided. Japanese companies have survived these difficult times by carefully reducing their operating costs: by thorough rationalization of their operations; by tighter than ever budgeting and control of expenditure; by further improvements in productivity; and by shifting the burden of part of their operational costs onto their affiliated companies and/or subcontractors.

The question of whether this strategy is right or wrong is not at issue here. What is important is that American and European corporations should understand the approach of Japanese businessmen to crisis management. In the words of Mr Misawa, president of Misawa Homes, one of the most successfully acquisition-minded companies in Japan:

When we acquire a company, we will fully guarantee the continued employment of all employees of that company. We have to do that at least. We will be willing to increase their salaries by as much as 50%, if we have to do so in order to give them some incentive. But if we do this, sure, we will at the same time double their workload.

American and European corporations should keep this underlying principle in mind.

All this does not mean, however, that Japanese companies would never dream of curtailing the workforce of an acquired company for cost reduction purposes. In fact, various curtailment measures, some of which are unique to Japan, may be taken. These include early retirement, often accompanied by increased retirement benefits and/or assistance in finding new jobs, deferring recruitment schedules, transferring employees to affiliated companies or subsidiaries, and forming new subsidiaries to generate new business and absorb the excess workforce.

8.5 LESSONS FROM THE READER'S DIGEST CASE

The complete closure of Reader's Digest Japan, which ceased to be a going concern in January 1986 after accumulating deficits of ¥3,929 million, is still very fresh in people's memories. Although the true reason for the company's failure was never made public, it was generally put down to failure of the American style of management. The employees of the company became unionized in 1956. According to a magazine report, the president of Reader's Digest Japan, who had been sent from the American parent company, implemented a labor management policy that involved conceding to labor union demands as much as possible, rather than suffering labor disputes.

It was reported that the parent company was eager to pursue short-term profits rather than the long-term growth of their Japanese subsidiary. In line with this policy, the union's extravagant claims were conceded to one after another: this included the adoption of a revolutionary new wage structure that guaranteed the same wage to all employees of the same age, regardless of their respective lengths of service or abilities; and an excessively generous special leave of absence system, allowing female employees lengthy periods of maternity leave. Predictably, this increased the company labor costs considerably, seriously eroding profitability.

Had Reader's Digest Japan been a purely Japanese company, it is probable that the labor unions would not have made such unreasonably excessive claims. And a management consisting solely of Japanese executives would not have been so submissive in their response. The fatal error at Reader's Digest Japan was the lack of understanding between labor and management that they were in the same boat, and that too heavy a financial load would lead to one inevitable result – the boat would sink. This joint understanding is very important in Japan, where lifetime employment with one company often prevails.

Although a number of local Japanese subsidiaries of American companies use, in their personnel management, a system of individual merits borrowed from their parent companies, few of these systems operate smoothly. American businessmen often criticize the Japanese style of management as irresponsible; and the "bottom-up" system of decision-making, discussed in detail in Section 5.8.1, may well deserve this tag, in the sense that no individual is ever blamed for an unfortunate corporate decision. But this system works both ways: while an individual employee is unlikely to be blamed if his decision turns out to have been wrong, he is equally unlikely to be promoted if his decision turns out to have been right! The American maxim "The buck stops here" is no longer relevant: responsibility is shared by everyone.

Another phenomenon often seen in Japanese companies owned by American or European investors or corporations is that Japanese employees who have skills in English or a European language often receive favorable treatment in terms of entrance examinations, salaries, and/or promotions. This kind of discrimination tends to create friction amongst the Japanese workers, and it demoralizes otherwise highly talented people who happen to have no particular linguistic ability – so much so that they sometimes seek alternative employment. According to a magazine report, Reader's Digest Japan used to operate in this way, and the ridiculous wage structure referred to above was adopted at the union's request precisely to prevent discrimination on grounds of linguistic ability.

In Osaka, there is a Japanese subsidiary of a certain American chemical company, which has been unprofitably engaged in the manufacture and marketing of chemical products in Japan for over ten years: in that time it has accumulated deficits of over ¥10 billion. The subsidiary's extremely poor performance is widely believed to be at least partly attributable to the fact that the American parent company has replaced the president of its Japanese subsidiary every two or three years. Furthermore, on each occasion a new American president has been appointed, with an American secretary, neither of whom has had any knowledge of the Japanese language. This has made it necessary for the subsidiary to hire an additional, bilingual secretary for its president. How could an American or European corporation with such a poor concept of management possibly run a Japanese subsidiary efficiently?

8.6 PERSONNEL ADMINISTRATION ERRORS MAY PROVE FATAL

In practice, it is very difficult for a foreign-capital-based Japanese company, particularly a new one, to hire fresh graduates from well-known, first-class colleges and universities. Most Japanese university students, particularly those from the best universities, prefer to be employed by first-class fully Japanese companies. Very few of them are prepared to accept employment with foreign-capital-based Japanese companies, no matter how large and well known their parent companies may be, unless they are leaders in their particular field, with a proven track record in Japan of a quarter century or more. One benefit of acquiring a top Japanese company is that the new American or European owner is unlikely to be disadvantaged with regard to recruitment. However, in order to retain this advantage there should be no rush to sweep away the established systems of recruitment, promotion, and merits evaluation, in favor of a more familiar system used in the new owner's home country.

As mentioned earlier in this chapter, and elsewhere, it is advisable for American and European corporations to make the least possible changes in the existing management teams of acquired Japanese companies, in order to ensure smooth and efficient operation. If, for some unavoidable reason, the president has to be replaced, an attempt should be made to find a suitable Japanese successor, in order to assure close communications between the management and the employees, and so as not to demoralize the latter. If this is not possible, then the preferred next choice is a non-Japanese candidate who has been resident in Japan for some years, and who appreciates Japanese society, culture, and ways of thinking, and the economy, business, and organizational systems and labor practices of Japanese companies. The worst possible choice, likely to cause serious friction between management and labor, would be to send as a replacement a new business-school graduate from overseas.

8.7 HOW TO RECRUIT HIGHLY TALENTED PEOPLE

Because of Japan's tradition of lifetime employment, which means that few businessmen change their employers – particularly at top management level – it is virtually impossible to find truly talented businessmen to fill top positions on the open labor market in Japan. Perhaps the best way to find them is through personal or business connections. Traditionally, major financial institutions, particularly banks and securities companies, major trading houses, and the national government have been the major sources of supply of people of this calibre. As mentioned in Section 5.2, Japanese commercial banks have long been supplying their personnel to clients to serve as top managers. The banks have the ability to do this because of their long tradition of annual graduate recruitment, usually taking a number of top-class graduates from the best universities.

Most of the people who have come out of national government agencies (such as the Ministries of Finance, International Trade and Industry, Foreign Affairs, Transportation, Telecommunications, and Health and Public Welfare) have been "Career Officials," employees who have passed the High-class Government Officials Qualification Examination. A significant number of such officials have recently left government employment at around 50 years of age – before their normal retirement age – to join the business world. Most of these accept employment with major companies, or with semigovernmental corporations, as board members, vice-chairmen, or executive vice-presidents. At least a few Career Officials have recently accepted employment with foreign-capital-based Japanese companies, in the role of president.

8.8 AVOID SHUTTING DOWN OR SELLING OFF

It is generally considered to be against business ethics in Japan to acquire a company and then resell the same company in small fragments to make rapid capital gains. Those indulging in such practices are contemptuously referred to as "corporation destroyers" or "destroying raiders." Therefore it is best to avoid having to shut down any operations, or sell divisions or factories, shortly after completing the acquisition of a Japanese company. Unavoidable sales and closures should be deferred for as long as possible, and then carried out piecemeal rather than all at once.

There have, of course, been some cases in Japan in which closures or sales have followed shortly after acquisitions; however, the companies concerned were invariably almost bankrupt, and the action formed part of a rescue plan. Any American or European corporation hoping to make a quick buck in this way is bound to damage its corporate image and good name in Japan.

Conclusion:
The Way Forward

The acquisition of an existing Japanese company is perhaps the quickest way for those American and European corporations that desire an active presence in Japan to achieve their objectives. However, such corporations must realize that this enterprise will require substantially more patience and more time and effort, and will call for the formulation of substantially more delicate step-by-step psychological tactics than it would in the US or Europe.

While seated around the negotiating table, they must always exercise the utmost care to pay their opponent or target company due respect, and to avoid the use of improper and offensive terminology – remember that the words "acquisition," "control," "buy-out," and "takeover" are taboo at an early stage.

They should also remember that the presence of their legal counsels during the early stages of the negotiation will be regarded as threatening or, again, offensive.

The virtual certainty that the rigid application of Western strategies and tactics in Japan will end in miserable and catastrophic failure cannot be stressed highly enough. The successful acquisition of a Japanese company calls for careful adaptation of familiar strategies, in which the assistance of reliable Japanese commercial banks, securities firms, and lawyers is invaluable. In conclusion, patience, time, and effort are the essential watchwords.

Index

220

Index

Heiwa Sogo Bank   16, 77, 78, 84, 85, 119
hidden assets   65–7
hidden liabilities   144–5
Hilton Hotels Group   120
Hirano Metals   106
Hirose, Mr Tokutaro   93
Hiroshima Bus Company   196, 199
Hiroshima Electric Railways Company   196, 199
Hitachi   192
Hochiki Co. Ltd   97–8
Hokkaido Can Manufacturing Company   196
Hokko Electronics Co. Ltd   86
Hokuto Audio Engineering   101
holding company   29, 193–4
    definition   193
    prohibition of   193–4
Hong Kong   191–3
hostile tender offers   162–6

Ibuki, Mr Kazuo   41
Iino Shipping Co. Ltd   66
Imperial Government of Japan   118
Industrial Bank of Japan   38, 93
Information Development Group   107
intangible assets   71–4
interlocking directorships, restrictions on   198–9
Interlubke system kitchen units   80
investment advisers   108
investment bank   198
Ishii Iron Works   106
Ishii Precision Tools Co. Ltd   46, 162

JAFCO   40
Janome Sewing Machines Company   42
Japacs Corporation   84
Japan National Railways Corporation   114
Japan Oil Transportation Company   195
Japan Railways   114
Japan Steel Corporation   77, 159
Jidosha Kiki Company   170–1
Jujiya   106
JUSCO   99

Kajima Construction   106
Kamaishi and Wanishi Steel Mills   118
Kanefutaura and Kyushu Steel Mills   118
Kanegafuchi Chemical Industries Corporation   86, 87

Kanemori Co. Ltd   148, 149
Kansai Sogo Bank   103
Kansai Steamship Company   81
Katakura Industries vs. *a Hong Kong investor*   191–3
Kawai Musical Instruments Company   195
Kawashima Textile   106
Keiaisha   170
Keiyo Screw Co. Ltd   33
Koa Oil   192
Kobayashi Pharmaceutical Industry Co. Ltd   96
Kokudo Keikaku Co. Ltd   66
Kokusai kigyo baishu handbook   ix
Kokusai Kogyo Corporation   113
Koromo no shita kara yoroi ga mieru   124
Kubota   125
Kurosawa Group   114
Kurushima Dock Group   80–2
Kyocera   83, 178
Kyoritsu Yakuhin Co. Ltd   8, 9, 32
Kyoto Ceramic   83
Kyowa Bank   125

labor layoff   210
labor relations   138–42, 210
labor unions   102–3, 138–42, 213
language skills   213–14
Large Retail Stores Restrictions Act   82
largest shareholder status   93–8, 126–31
law of contract   191
lawyers, role of   108–9
leave of absence   213
Legal Affairs Bureau (MOJ)   11
legal rights   131–4
Liberal Democratic Party   29
licensed tax consultants   203
LIFE   106
lifetime employment   215–16
liquidation profit   207
listing requirements   161
Long-Term Credit Bank of Japan   38, 170
long-term perspective   210–12
losing face   52
loyalty   209

Mamiya cameras   80
management team   100–2, 209, 215
Martini Rossi S.p.A.   34
Maruzen   119
maternity leave   213
Matsui Construction   106
Matsuya   106

222

Index

Index

Nisseki Housing Industries Co. Ltd 45
Nisshin Oil Mills Ltd 96
Nissho Guiken 95
Nissho Iwai 160
Nittetsu Curtain Walls Co. Ltd 76, 100, 159
Nittetsu Sash Sales 101
Nohmi Bosai Kogyo Co. Ltd 98
Nomura Securities Co. Ltd 22, 40, 108, 148
nonfloating share ratio 155
notification for proposed acquisition of shares 184–7

occupying force syndrome 102
OECD 190
Okamura Corporation 66
Oki Electric 106
Okinawa Electric Power Company 171, 172
Okuma Machinery Works 102
Okuma, Mr Takeo 102–3
Okuno Machinery Works Co. Ltd 14
Okuno, Mr Toshikazu 14
Okura Trading 106
Orient Finance 106
Orient Leasing Co. Ltd 98, 101, 115
Oriental Hotel Company 82
Osaka Buildings 106
Osaka Ichioka Co. Ltd 98
Osaka Oxygen 106, 157
Osaka Steamship Co. Ltd 119
Osaka Wheels Mfg. Company 78
Osano, Mr Kenji 113
Osawa & Co. Ltd 16, 80
ownership of corporations 89–90

package deal 99
Parent Corporation 27
PCSE ratio 157, 158
personnel administration 214–15
Photonics Stock Ownership Association 94
PIPS 79
Plus Corporation 83
Pogenpohl system kitchen units 80
post-acquisition management 209–17
press releases 135–6
price book ratio (PBR) 65
price earning ratio (PER) 63
prior notification 183–9, 200
    consequences of not filing 191–3
procedural requirements 183–9
promissory notes 144–5
proxy solicitation 173–7

Prudential Asia Investment Corporation 34
public disclosures 135–6
purchase of business or assets, restrictions on 181–2, 201–2
    use of term 11
purchase of newly issued stock by private placement 166–9
purchase of stock from major shareholders 159–62

R&D 18, 22, 48, 50, 55, 125
Rawpack Corporation 34
Reader's Digest Japan 212–14
Reagan Administration 71
recruitment
    of highly talented people 215–16
    problems of 214–15
Regional Finance Bureau 174
registered securities 162
Representative Director 182
Riccar Corporation 15, 81–2, 143
ringuisho 129
Rorer Group Inc. 8, 32
Rorer Japan Inc. 9
Rules Governing the Solicitation of Proxies in Relation to Listed Shares 174
Ryosan 106

Sagami Denki Co. Ltd 32
Saitama Bank 42
Saitama Silver Seiko Co. 83
Sakurada Machinery 106
sales outlets 67–71
San'a Pharmaceutical 32
Sankyo 192
Sankyo Seiki 36, 103, 123, 136, 141, 148, 157
Sanoyas 106
Sanritsu Automation Co. Ltd 95
Sanwa Bank 106
Sanyo Electric 125, 156
Schlumberger Japan 120
Schlumberger Ltd 120
SECOM Co. Ltd 97–8, 106
secrecy maintenance 135–6
Securities Bureau 122
securities business, definition 197–8
securities companies 108
Securities and Exchange Act 23, 122, 123, 142, 162–5, 167, 174, 197
securities transfer tax 203
Seibu Department Stores 80
Seibu Group 80, 81
Seibu Railway Group 66

224

Index

Index

226